A HANDBOOK OF
GEMSTONES & JEWELRY

A HANDBOOK OF
GEMSTONES & JEWELRY

revealing the magic . . . unveiling the mystique

by Nancy and Al Benedict

St. Petersburg, Florida

We extend our deep appreciation to those who encouraged us to write this handbook and without whose assistance its completion would not have been possible. For their time, their support, and their faith in our efforts, we are sincerely grateful to:

Bruce Watters, Inc., Registered Jewelers, American Gem Society, St. Petersburg, Florida

Ellen B. Taylor, GIA, Rx Gold Doctor, St. Petersburg, Florida

Sue and Jack Hazelden, Lapidaries, St. Petersburg, Florida

Leona and Hugh Sheffield, St. Petersburg, Florida

Steve Clayton, Clayton Lapidary, Etc., St. Petersburg, Florida

For their benevolent assistance, we also extend special thanks to:

Roger S. Trontz, Gemstones, Jupiter, Florida

Ari Reith, P. Gems, New York, New York

Gladys Swigert, St. Petersburg, Florida and Queensbury, New York

Photographs by Sidney Wilson of Sidney Wilson Photography, St. Petersburg, Florida

Cover art and illustrations by Douglas J. Ponte, Tampa, Florida

We are most grateful to Sidney and Doug for their professionalism and their superb artistic talents.

Copyright © 1996 by Nancy Eleanor and Alfred Payden Benedict.

International Standard Book Number: 0-9652510-0-4

Library of Congress Catalog Card Number: 96-96390

Printed in the United States of America by Gohrs Printing Service, Inc., Erie, Pennsylvania

To all who love and admire
the beauty, charm, and magic of
gemstones and jewelry

CONTENTS

CONTENTS (Continued)

PREFACE

Since the dawn of civilization, mankind has carried on a passionate love affair with gemstones, jewelry, and precious metals. This bond of affection and admiration has intensified with the passing of time. The number of natural gems has increased and, with the advent of synthetic stones and the creation of fashion jewelry, the choices are, indeed, staggering. Purchasing a beautiful piece of jewelry is a grand adventure, and wearing that special piece never ceases to bring pleasure.

The gemstones now cherished throughout the world have and, undoubtedly, will continue to spread their aura of magic and mystique. At one time, they represented nobility, wealth, and power. They were at the center of superstition and, later, religion. They reached out to the universe and even to the depths of elaborate burial chambers. Today, gemstones abound with folklore. They were once ground into small particles and ingested as medicinal agents. In the Middle Ages, great master painters ground gems to use as pigmentation in many of their spectacular works of art.

Gems, jewelry, and precious metals remain a source of fascination in nearly every culture. Although jewelry manufacturing is a multibillion dollar industry worldwide, many jewelry lovers have limited knowledge of this interesting, even intriguing, realm of beauty, elegance, and grace. This handbook is intended not only to increase knowledge but also to provide pleasure.

INTRODUCTION

Since the early mists of time, gemstones, jewelry, and precious metals have been a focal point of civilization. The beauty, brilliance, and glamour, especially of gemstones, have fascinated nearly all mankind and have held a prominent place in every aspect of human life, even unto the grave.

Gemstones were key symbols of royalty and nobility, of power and wealth, of religious import, and of beauty and romance. But symbolism did not end there. From the belief that gems were linked to the sun, the moon, and the universe, today's treasured birthstones and zodiac stones most likely evolved.

The dazzling beauty of gemstones and the magic of their colors inspire a sense of the supernatural. Their mystique creates a burning desire in both men and women to own and display these tantalizing gifts of nature. They bring as much delight as seeing that special sunrise or sunset, a pastel rainbow after a storm, or the flaming beauty of autumn in New England.

For many centuries, gemstones were believed to hold the extraordinary powers of protecting and curing, and they played a major role in the lives of all classes of individuals who wore them as amulets and talismans.

That magic has never waned. Gemstones are as popular today as they were at any time in recorded history, and their popularity will surely continue into the future.

To this day, many consider gems as prudent investments. During war or economic crisis, some convert their assets into jewelry, since jewelry is easy to transport and fairly easy to redeem for cash.

Jewelry has had a profound effect on countless civilizations and cultures. Since antiquity, this style and method of adornment was found throughout Asia, Australia, Europe, and Africa as well as in the Americas. During medieval times in black Africa, skilled craftsmen produced superb jewelry.

What prompted us to write this handbook? First, as ardent lovers of gems, jewelry, and precious metals, we were convinced of the need for simple, concise, easily understood narratives about these fascinating subjects. Second, we thought that others who share our enthusiasm would like to know certain interesting facts simply for the joy of knowing. Buying a piece of jewelry should be an experience that evokes pleasure and satisfaction. Being equipped with sufficient knowledge can help ensure success in this magical adventure.

We believe the information in this handbook will answer many questions and will simplify matters that may have been somewhat confusing. But don't be afraid to ask more questions when purchasing any kind of jewelry. If it is gemstone jewelry, some questions you may want to ask yourself are: Is the stone(s) the type, shape, size and, especially, the color I want? Can I afford it? Does it have pizzazz? If the answer to each of these is a resounding yes, you should derive much enjoyment from your selection for many years.

THE SCIENCE OF GEMOLOGY

Millions of people worldwide have a deep fascination with and appreciation of gemstones and precious metals. By far, the more complex of these two areas is that of gems. So complex that it has, over the centuries, developed into the science of gemology. The science has not been restricted to minerals but includes organic matter such as pearls, coral, and ivory. It transcends natural gemstones and includes stones that are treated as well as those that are synthetic or artificial. Gemology has become so all-encompassing that it would be nearly impossible to name and describe every gem within every family and to explain each aspect of this complex subject.

Simply defined, gemology is an old and venerated field of science. Since ancient times, it has had established rules and guidelines, which include standards, nomenclature, and even naming many newly discovered gems. The terminology alone is a good example of the need to maintain orderly conduct in the massive gemstone industry. Some of the many gemology terms and their definitions are as follows:

❖ GEMSTONES

An all-inclusive word for ornamental stones. Many gemologists have de-emphasized the terms *precious* and *semiprecious*, since all gems are considered precious, especially to their owners.

❖ JEWELRY

Every piece used for personal adornment, whether pure, altered, or imitated, is classified as jewelry.

❖ CRYSTAL

Solid matter, of a crystalline structure, displaying orderly atomic arrangement.

❖ MINERAL

A natural substance; a mixture of inorganic compounds.

❖ STONES

The name given to all solid constituents of the earth's crust. In the world of jewelry, a stone is a gem or gemstone.

Some specific terms relating to the clarity or clearness of gems are:

❖ TRANSPARENT

Light moves through the stone with little distortion.

❖ TRANSLUCENT

Light is transmitted but is diffused and cloudy.

❖ OPAQUE

Transmits no light whatsoever.

GEMS BY COLOR

A major consideration when purchasing gemstone jewelry is *color*. One selects from a multitude of hues and shades, since *precise* colors are not found in nature's brilliant stones. The following chart lists some gemstones found in various hues and shades of the more prevalent colors.

COLOR	GEMSTONES
Red/Pink	ruby, garnet, pink sapphire, zircon, scapolite, beryl, coral, kunzite, quartz, diamond, onyx, morganite, spinel, carnelian
Orange	sapphire, topaz, spinel, zircon, tourmaline, fire opal, beryl, garnet, jade, onyx, coral
Yellow	citrine, beryl, sapphire, topaz, diamond, moonstone, amber, andalusite, diopside, zircon, jade, quartz, scapolite, garnet
Green	emerald, garnet, serpentine, tourmaline, peridot, zircon, alexandrite, sapphire, diamond, aventurine, turquoise, jade, malachite, diopside, bloodstone, topaz, andalusite, beryl
Blue	sapphire, tanzanite, spinel, aquamarine, topaz, zircon, quartz, turquoise, lapis lazuli, sodalite, diamond, azurite, iolite, coral, chalcedony, moonstone
Violet	amethyst, sapphire, spinel, iolite, kunzite, tanzanite, scapolite, topaz

GEMSTONES

Agate Geode

Agate

Alexandrite

Amber

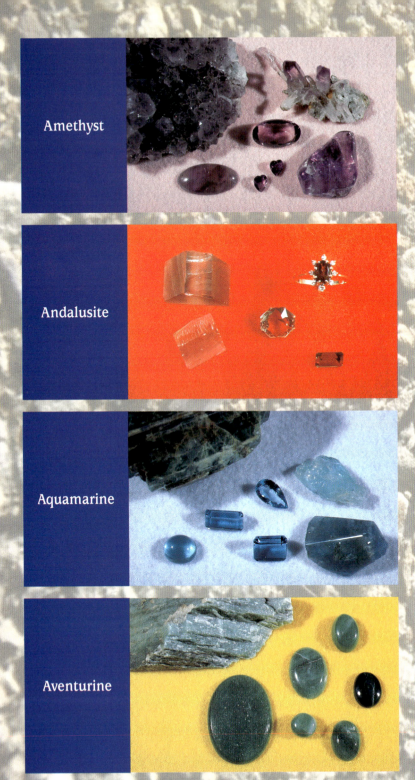

Amethyst

Andalusite

Aquamarine

Aventurine

Azur-malachite

Beryl
(Golden Beryl)

Beryl
(Morganite)

Bloodstone

Carnelian

Chalcedony

Citrine

Coral

Cubic Zirconia

Diamond

Diopside

Emerald

Garnet

Iolite

Jade

Jasper

Kunzite

Lapis Lazuli

Malachite

Marcasite

Moonstone

Onyx

Opal

Pearl

14

Peridot

Quartz

Rose
Quartz

Smoky
Quartz

Ruby

Sapphire

Scapolite

Serpentine

16

Sodalite

Spinel

Tanzanite

Topaz
(Blue/Colorless)

Topaz (Golden)

Tourmaline

Turquoise

Zircon

INTRODUCTION TO GEMSTONES

Gemstones are one of the more radiant gifts nature has bestowed on mankind. Every gem transmits a clear and personal gift of unparalleled beauty to the beholder. Above all, gemstones render a natural expression of individual style and demeanor.

Although some still use the term *colored gemstones*, many radiant and stunning gems are colorless. More and more, we refer to all gems, whether they have or do not have color, simply as gems, stones, or gemstones.

For centuries, diamonds, emeralds, rubies, and sapphires were classified as precious, while all other gems were classified as semiprecious. But in recent times, because of the rarity, cost, beauty, and popularity of so many brilliant stones once categorized as semiprecious, we have downplayed these labels. To the true lover of gemstones, every one is special and every one is precious.

In the final analysis, we buy gems for four basic reasons: beauty, durability, rarity, and value.

AGATE

COLOR: layered, streaked, or banded in various colors
MOHS' HARDNESS: 6.5 - 7

Agate dates back to ancient times and has been highly regarded, especially by north Africans, for centuries. The stone is classified as a chalcedony and, occasionally, includes varying amounts of opal. Agates are usually dyed to obtain their brilliant coloration, an art known to the Romans in imperial times. Today, the procedure used for dying agates is a closely guarded secret.

Egyptians used agate for rings, seals, cameos, drinking vessels, and charm necklaces. Today, the stone is used for these items as well as for brooches, pendants, bracelets, and objects of art, with many agate jewelry pieces being manufactured in Germany.

Through the centuries, and even to this day, agate has been valued for its unusual markings and brilliant colors. The stone was believed to ensure that the wearer would be agreeable, persuasive, and favored by the gods. Agate assured victory in battle and guarded its wearer from all dangers. Wearing agate ornaments was also believed to cure insomnia and assure pleasant dreams.

Whether the positive attributes associated with this stone are simply folklore or whether they are fact, agate amulets are worn even to this day. In past centuries, the owner of an amulet could set an extravagant purchase price, especially in north Africa. Agates set in antique jewelry are of major interest to collectors.

Agate is fragile and requires extra care in cleaning as well as a protective setting for the stone. When purchasing this gem, you should determine if the color is natural. If the stone is dyed, it could be less valuable.

ALEXANDRITE

COLOR: green in daylight; light red in artificial light
MOHS' HARDNESS: 8.5

Alexandrite, a member of the chrysoberyl family, is a fascinating and coveted gem, although one of the more costly. Alexandrite has the unique capability of changing from green in daylight to light red in artificial light.

This stone, discovered in Russia 150 years ago, was named after Czar Alexander II. Because of its fairly recent discovery, this gemstone has acquired limited folklore; however, it is considered a stone of only *good* omen and is highly regarded as a talisman. The largest alexandrite to be cut weighs 66 carats and is displayed in the Smithsonian Institution in Washington, D.C.

While somewhat available in smaller sizes, alexandrite has become scarce in sizes of three or more carats. In recent years, an excellent synthetic alexandrite has been created, and some simulated versions are difficult to distinguish from genuine stones. You would be wise, therefore, to have the authenticity of your alexandrite verified.

Although alexandrite is a hard gemstone, it is sensitive to certain chemicals and other abrasives and should be protected from hard knocks. Be cautious when caring for and maintaining this stone.

AMBER

COLOR: various shades of yellow to brown, red, blue, black, and nearly colorless
MOHS' HARDNESS: 2 - 2.5

Amber, which is fossilized tree sap, must be at least a million years old to be genuine. Documents indicate, however, that some amber may have formed as long as 50 million years ago. As tree sap hardened, bugs, leaves, and other natural sediments became encased within. In fact, the result of this phenomenon greatly enhances the value of an amber piece. Amber is called the *Gold of the North* because its major source is the Baltic Sea. Some amber floats up from the bottom of the sea and, after storms, large chunks wash up on the shores of neighboring countries.

Amber has been used as amulets and various other decorations since the Stone Age when cavemen and women may have worn it. For thousands of years, the Chinese used amber for medicines, perfumes, and incense. Probably the first material ever used for jewelry and religious objects, amber is a tough substance even though it is lightweight. As a result of its beautiful colors and the ease with which it can be fashioned, amber remains a favorite object of adornment.

Many myths have evolved from the much-loved amber. In early Grecian times, it was believed that, as the sun set, a portion of it melted to form the amber left on the ocean floor. And the Chinese believed that, when a tiger died, its spirit penetrated the earth to become amber. The Roman Emperor Nero was said to have loved the gemstone because it matched the color of his wife's hair. He frequently ordered his troops to return with as much amber as they could find.

Besides its many natural colors, amber can also be dyed. Imitation amber is often made of plastic; however, when genuine amber is dropped into a salt solution it will float, while plastic imitations will not. Additionally, genuine amber will start to emit heat when it is rubbed. In fact, it was said to have been used, in prehistoric times, to conduct electricity.

Remember that amber **must** be worn often and should be

cleaned only with water. And be aware that if it is left in a dark place such as a box or drawer, for extended periods of time, amber will crack.

AMETHYST

COLOR: pale violet to deep purple
MOHS' HARDNESS: 7

The color of royalty and power, amethyst has been highly valued since the dawn of civilization. A well-regarded member of the quartz family, this stunning gemstone is available in a moderate price range. Better quality stones are either faceted or cabochon cut for use in jewelry. When an amethyst geode is opened and determined to be of lesser quality but still beautiful, the pieces are used, for example, as book ends or other objects of art.

Today, an amethyst symbolizes love, truth, passion, sincerity, and hope. But this gem has acquired a rich legacy of mystique and was once thought to have extraordinary powers. In ancient times, the stone was believed to bring peace of mind by granting freedom from everyday concerns and controlling evil thoughts. Later, amethyst was believed to promote understanding.

This gemstone was also a symbol of piety and humility and was believed to bring good luck, protect the wearer from the evil eye, and prevent homesickness. Amethyst was once believed to ensure that the wearer would be safe from death by poison. Believing that the stone would prevent intoxication, the early Greeks carved wine goblets from amethyst.

One legend relates that the goddess Diana turned a fair maiden into stone to protect her from a tiger attack ordered by Bacchus, the Greek God of Wine. To repent for having unleashed his animals, Bacchus poured wine over the stone maiden, turning her into rich purple amethyst.

A buyer should be aware that amethysts are created synthetically today, and some are fine representations of genuine stones. Also, be aware that extended periods of heat or direct sun exposure could cause some genuine amethysts to fade; otherwise, they require little care or maintenance. If you use a commercial jewelry cleaner, read the directions carefully to ensure that the solution will not harm this gemstone.

ANDALUSITE

COLOR: various shades of yellow, brown, and green
MOHS' HARDNESS: 7.5

In the past, andalusite was of interest primarily to collectors but, in recent years, it has been used more frequently in fine jewelry pieces, especially men's rings. Andalusite is fairly hard and durable, adding to its appeal. The most interesting characteristic of the gem is its ability to emit several colors in various directions. Depending on its cut, the stone will perform this *magic* when placed at different angles.

One belief in ancient times, possibly because of andalusite's magical quality, was that green stones would cure eye ailments. In Spain, an andalusite believed to have great power is located at a religious shrine near the tomb of James the Apostle. Devout Christians venerate this gem, for the clear image of a cross can be seen within it.

An andalusite, weighing 28 carats, is housed at the Smithsonian Institution in Washington, D. C. At this time, however, these gemstones are not abundantly available on the open market.

Because of its hardness and durability, andalusite requires only normal care and maintenance.

AQUAMARINE

COLOR: various shades of blue and blue-green
MOHS' HARDNESS: 7.5 - 8

From the Latin for sea water, aquamarine was named for its blue and blue-green ocean colors. The most desirable stone is one that is a clear, brilliant blue. Although this exquisite gem is brittle, it is not *as* brittle as its counterpart the emerald, also a member of the beryl family. Fine quality aquamarines are available in smaller stones, but they are expensive; larger "aquas" have become scarce in recent years, and these are quite costly.

In ancient times, sailors wore these gemstones as talismans, believing that, because the colorations were those of the sea, they would be protected from storms. The gem was also believed to have a calming effect, as does the sound of the sea, a belief held by many even today.

Dreaming about an aquamarine is interpreted to mean that happiness is in store. The stone is believed to preserve the marriage of its wearer and, additionally, to stimulate the intellect. These magnificent gems represent youth, hope, and good health and offer special blessings to those whose birthdays are in March.

Although synthetic aquamarines have been created, most are not of good quality and, therefore, have not become popular. A buyer should be aware that the beautiful blue topaz, while similar in color, is of much less value.

Because aquamarines are brittle, they require extra care when cleaning and handling. Read jewelry cleaner directions carefully to ensure that the solution can be used for these gemstones.

AVENTURINE

COLOR: iridescent in shades of green and brown
MOHS' HARDNESS: 7

Aventurine, a member of the quartz family, is a durable gemstone, enhanced by tiny flecks of mica that sparkle from within. Because the gemstone was accidentally discovered, it received its name from the French word *aventure,* meaning accident. Modestly priced, this gem is popular in the United States as well as in southeast and southern Asia, especially India.

This stone is used for decorative objects of art and cabochon cut for rings, earrings, and bracelets. The gemstone is also used for various shaped beads that are fashioned into jewelry such as necklaces, pendants, and pins. These pieces highly complement many of today's fashions.

Aventurine was prominent in Egyptian religion, as evidenced by aventurine beads, amulets, and seals found in the tombs of the great Pharaohs. Since that time, this stone, along with others such as carnelian and malachite, has been carved into scarabs for jewelry. Whether set in gold or silver, these fascinating scarabs are often part of a collection.

A scarab beetle was considered sacred by the ancient Egyptians who wore carved scarabs as talismans. Many of these have been preserved and are located in museums throughout the world. Today, scarabs are representations of those ancient talismans once worn to symbolize the sun, the soul, immortality, and resurrection.

A buyer should be aware that good glass imitations abound. Genuine aventurine requires little care or maintenance and needs only to be polished with a soft, dry cloth.

AZURITE

COLOR: dark blue
MOHS' HARDNESS: 3.5 - 4

Azurite, like malachite, has been used as a gemstone since ancient times and is found in copper deposits. Occasionally, these two gems become interwoven to form a dazzling azur-malachite. Although azurite has a brilliant luster, it is usually not used in rings because of its softness. The stone is, however, often cabochon cut for use in jewelry pieces such as beads, bracelets, and pendants. Azurite is also carved and highly polished for decorative art objects.

A note of caution. Immersing azurite in ammonia or cleaning it with any product containing ammonia could destroy this gem's beauty, the same as it could destroy the beauty of malachite. Only normal care and maintenance is required for this stone; simply clean it with a soft, dry cloth.

A potential buyer of lapis lazuli should be aware that some azurite closely resembles the more costly lapis.

BERYL

COLOR: an extensive variety of mostly soft colors
MOHS' HARDNESS: 7.5 - 8

Beryl is found in a variety of colors, including pink, orange, yellow, green, blue, red, brown, and colorless. Some of the more popular gemstones from the colorful beryl family are aquamarine, emerald, golden beryl, and morganite.

Many of these gemstones are transparent and, from antiquity through the Middle Ages, colorless beryl was used for eye glasses and as magnifying lenses. Beryl was believed to provide its wearer with help against enemies in battle. This gem was also believed then, as it is today, to promote friendliness, intelligence, and hard work. According to legend, beryl reawakens a married couple's love in later years.

Although gems of the beryl group are resistant to most chemicals and other abrasives, these stones, especially emeralds, are brittle and can easily be damaged. Therefore, ensure they are in protective settings and be cautious in their care and maintenance.

Golden Beryl

COLOR: various shades of yellow

Morganite

Although golden beryl and morganite have been known only in recent times, they have grown in popularity. Along with their moderate costs, both gemstones have excellent clarity and brilliance as well as durability, resulting in the creation of magnificent jewelry pieces. Golden beryl of the orange variety is often heated to produce the far more popular pink morganite. A golden beryl, with a cat's eye effect, has a silvery-white streak of light across a curved surface.

BLOODSTONE (Heliotrope)

The deep green bloodstone, also known as heliotrope, is chalcedony flecked with red jasper. Most desirable when its jasper fibers are well-defined, bloodstone is relatively inexpensive and popular for use in men's jewelry, especially signet rings. Much folklore has evolved from this ancient stone probably because, when it is highly polished, the red spots look like drops of blood. One legend relates that the spots represented the blood of Christ.

Since the days of classical Greece, the bloodstone has generated many myths. Throughout history, this gem has held a prominent place, and was considered to be a strong curative. When worn as an amulet, bloodstone was believed to stop bleeding and to serve as an antidote for snake bites and a remedy for urinary diseases. In ancient times and during the Middle Ages, the gem was worn to prevent sun stroke and protect against the evil eye. The stone was further believed to be especially protective of men.

Bloodstone is a hard and durable gem, requiring little care or maintenance. Simply clean it with a jewelry polishing cloth.

CARNELIAN

COLOR: pale to deep red and reddish-brown
MOHS' HARDNESS: 6.5 - 7

Carnelian, a variety of chalcedony, is fairly durable and moderate in cost. The stone is often found in antique jewelry and is used today for cameos and scarabs as well as for carving figurines and bowls. The reddish colors of carnelian, which is either cabochon cut for rings and various other jewelry pieces or tumbled for bracelets and necklaces, enhance many of today's fashions. Those who are timid favor this gemstone because it is believed to bestow courage and boldness.

We know this gem has been used for thousands of years because two carnelian necklaces were found on a mummy, of great nobility, that had been entombed in an Egyptian burial chamber circa 3500 B.C. According to one legend, Napoleon found a carnelian on an Egyptian battlefield and, for the rest of his life, wore the stone said to have been engraved with the following: *THE SLAVE ABRAHAM RELYING UPON THE MERCIFUL.* This gemstone was also highly regarded by Moslems because, according to another legend, Muhammad wore a carnelian-engraved ring that he used as a seal.

Although carnelians require little care or maintenance, exercise caution to protect these stones, since some are more fragile than others.

CHALCEDONY

COLOR: various shades of white, gray, and blue; for other members of this group, a variety of colors
MOHS' HARDNESS: 6.5 - 7

Chalcedony, a member of the quartz family, is a hard, durable stone, which is gaining in popularity. Included in this family are gems such as agate, jasper, carnelian, chrysoprase, bloodstone, and a bluish variety of chalcedony. These are found in various shades of many colors and most are translucent, but some milkier varieties are opaque.

While many of the stones in this group are used in their natural states, chalcedony is porous and can be easily dyed. This gem is polished to a high luster and used for objects of art. Cabochon-cut stones are used for jewelry pieces such as necklaces, bracelets, earrings, and brooches. Substantial deposits are found worldwide, contributing to its moderate cost.

In ancient times, chalcedony was popular throughout the Mediterranean, and sailors wore amulets to protect them from drowning. In the Middle Ages, the gem was worn as a talisman to avert depression and ward off *phantoms of the night.*

Chalcedony requires only normal care and maintenance. Simply polish it with a soft, dry cloth.

CITRINE

COLOR: pale to dark yellow
MOHS' HARDNESS: 7

Citrine, a member of the quartz family, is an ancient stone that was highly prized in classical Greece. At that time, the stone was known as burnt amethyst, most likely because much citrine is produced by heat-treating purple amethyst, also of the quartz group. The durable citrine, its contemporary name, is sometimes mistaken for golden topaz, which is less available and more costly. In fact, citrine is now considered by many as the November birthstone, probably because it is modestly priced, strikingly beautiful, and more plentiful than the golden topaz.

This gemstone is usually faceted but sometimes cabochon cut for jewelry pieces such as rings, earrings, pendants, and bracelets. Some pieces are fashioned into beads for necklace strands and bracelets, while some are used for decorative objects of art.

In the past, citrine was believed to relieve shortness of breath, aid in digestion, prevent snake bites, control tempers, and calm the wearer. Additionally, the gem was said to prevent scandal and evil thoughts and inspire cheerfulness and hope.

Today, wearing a citrine is believed to improve a speaker's voice and, at the same time, help project a strong image. The stone is also believed to bring inner peace by uniting one's mind, emotions, and intuition.

Citrine requires little care or maintenance.

CORAL

COLOR: pink, red, white, blue, orange, and black
MOHS' HARDNESS: 3 - 4

An organic gem from the sea, coral is harvested with wire mesh nets dragged along the ocean floor. These formations can be found at depths from 10 to 1,000 feet and resemble small tree branches. Corals are found in a variety of bright colors, which result from the algae living in their tissues and producing their food. The rarest and most costly coral is **the noble red**, also called **blood red** today.

After coral is cleaned, cut, and carved, it is polished to a high luster. However, those in certain countries believe that, if coral is cut, it will lose its magical powers. Even today, many bracelets and necklaces are fashioned of uncut coral, or coral *in the rough*.

Amulets of coral, dating back to the time of Christ, were worn to cure madness, impart wisdom, calm storms, and prevent sterility. This gem was also believed to protect the wearer against blood disorders and assure safe passage to travelers. To this day, red coral signifies attachment and devotion.

Be advised that the color can and, in many instances, will fade when coral is exposed to the sun. Being a soft gem, it is sensitive to heat, hot solutions, and acids and, especially, to vinegar. Since glass, bone, and plastic imitations abound, exercise caution when purchasing coral.

CUBIC ZIRCONIA (CZ)

COLOR: colorless and various shades of various colors
MOHS' HARDNESS: 8.5 - 9

Cubic zirconia, commonly known as CZ, is the best diamond simulation to date. Many jewelers have had difficulty, at first glance, distinguishing a quality CZ from a genuine diamond. Almost as brilliant as a diamond, a fine cubic zirconia has great fire and is hard and durable. Carats are units of weight not only for diamonds and most other gemstones but also for CZs.

Cubic zirconia is produced today in various colors. A CZ of good quality will not fade with age and is an excellent alternative to a diamond, whether set in jewelry worn for informal or formal occasions. These stones are fashioned into beautiful pieces such as rings, earrings, pins, pendants, necklaces, and tennis bracelets. Wearing CZ jewelry, especially when traveling, will not cause as much concern for its monetary loss as would wearing genuine diamonds.

These stones require little care or maintenance. Quality CZs are an excellent choice for the luxury look of diamonds at a fraction of the cost.

DIAMOND

COLOR: black, blue, brown, colorless, green, red,
and yellow
MOHS' HARDNESS: 10

Today, as in the past, the diamond is the most coveted of

gemstones. Its brilliance, hardness, and fire are unsurpassed, and its beauty has been a source of fascination for thousands of years. Diamonds are found in a variety of colors, but colorless stones are, by far, the most popular; however, both yellow and coffee-colored stones have become quite popular in recent years. Composed of pure crystallized carbon, the structure of a diamond is the simplest of all gems.

Diamonds are almost always faceted, but only when cut to specific proportions is their true beauty released. These fiery stones are set into engagement rings and wedding bands as well as cocktail rings, earrings, pendants, tennis and other bracelets, brooches, and pins. Smaller colorless diamonds are often used to enhance colored gemstone pieces as well as watches.

The quality and value of a diamond are determined by **the four C's:** color, clarity, cut, and carat weight. Depending on personal taste and on the stone's purpose, certain "C's" may be more important than others.

Approximately ninety percent of the diamond trade is controlled through a central selling organization in London. Of the diamonds produced worldwide, fifty percent are sold in the United States; however, these gemstones have become increasingly popular throughout Europe and Japan. Surprisingly, eighty percent of all diamonds mined each year are used for industrial purposes, since they are not of gem quality.

Until the mid-19th century, a diamond was exclusively a man's stone, but today the gem is widely recognized as a symbol of love and betrothal. Ninety percent of today's prospective brides in the United States prefer diamond engagement rings. And many individuals buy diamonds solely as investments.

Since the diamond has played a significant role throughout history, much folklore has resulted, and many magical powers have been attributed to this superb gemstone. During ancient times in India, red and yellow diamonds were royal gems worn exclusively by kings. Later, a diamond was recognized as the emblem of fearlessness and invincibility, and the gem was believed to bestow superior strength and courage to the wearer. In the Middle Ages, the stone was worn as a talisman to enhance a husband's love for his wife. Even sexual prowess has been attributed to diamonds.

The largest uncut diamond ever found was the flawless Cullinan Diamond, which weighed 3,106 carats. From this immense stone, 105 others were cut, one of which was the Cullinan I, known as *the Star of Africa*. This pear-shaped beauty, weighing 530 carats, is among the British Crown Jewels on display in the Tower of London. The blue *Hope Diamond*, a "smaller" but more infamous stone weighing 44.5 carats, is housed at the Smithsonian Institution in Washington, D.C.

Because of its cutting resistance and hardness, a diamond can be used to cut another diamond, but it can also be chipped, or even broken, if it receives a hard blow from certain angles. Otherwise, this *gem of gems* requires little care or maintenance and, for the most part, is not sensitive to chemicals. Diamonds may be cleaned with most commercial jewelry solutions, including ultrasonic cleaners, which may be used safely for rubies, **diamonds**, and sapphires — red, **white**, and blue!

DIOPSIDE

COLOR: pale to dark green, colorless, gray, and yellow
MOHS' HARDNESS: 5.5 - 6.5

Diopside is a silicate belonging to the pyroxene family. Certain pieces of diopside with inclusions can be polished as a cat's eye or as a star diopside, but these are rare and costly. With the presence of iron, a dark chrome-green variety, or chromdiopside, is formed.

No myths or folklore have evolved from diopside but, in recent times, the beauty of this gemstone has increased its popularity for use in jewelry pieces.

Although relatively soft, the gem is durable and polishes well, requiring little care or maintenance.

EMERALD

COLOR: pale to dark green
MOHS' HARDNESS: 8

The emerald, while from the beryl family, is truly in a class of its own. Rich, brilliant green emeralds are highly prized, the most valuable stones being mined in South America. Flawless, transparent emeralds with excellent color cost more than diamonds of equal weight, but these gems are rare. Most are clouded by inclusions known as *jardin,* the French word for garden. These inclusions are undeniable evidence of an emerald's authenticity, and this characteristic is most helpful when differentiating between genuine and synthetic stones. Fine synthetic emeralds have been produced for many years and, as with genuine stones, they are quite expensive.

Even though emeralds are hard stones, they are brittle and will chip easily, requiring special care in setting, handling, and wearing. The emerald cut, with its four corners faceted to protect the stone, was developed specifically to prevent the sensitive emerald from chipping. Today, the emerald cut is used not only for this gem but for many others as well.

This stone was once believed to reveal the sincerity of a lover's words. When placed under the tongue, an emerald empowered its owner with the ability to predict the future. One legend relates that God gave King Solomon four precious stones, one of which was an emerald. By possessing these four gems, Solomon was endowed with power over all creation.

A genuine emerald was found in Babylonia as early as 4,000 B.C. But Cleopatra is said to have owned the earliest emerald mines near the Red Sea in Egypt. Julius Caesar is said to have collected emeralds, believing they warded off epilepsy and eye disease, both from which he suffered. Today, these dazzling gems represent faith and hope, spring and rebirth.

Most commercial jewelry cleaners should not be used for emeralds. Carefully clean these gemstones with a soft, dry cloth.

GARNET

COLOR: various shades of almost every color
       except blue
MOHS' HARDNESS: 6 to 7.5

Because these stones are available in almost every color

except blue, the garnet family is an exciting one in the gem world. From the Latin for pomegranate, the seeds of which the stone was thought to resemble, a garnet is hard, brilliant, and durable. Depending on its size and quality, the cost of this gem is moderate to high.

These gemstones have often been mistaken for those of more value, for example, the rich green *tsavorite*, a dazzling garnet, is sometimes mistaken for a fine quality emerald. In fact, a tsavorite garnet is more durable than an emerald, and some tsavorites are more brilliant. The rare green *demantoid* garnet is even more costly than a tsavorite and has more fire.

Garnets are more commonly found in various shades of red with slightly brown or violet tints, and some of these quality stones can be confused with rubies. The champagne-peach variety is known as a *grossular* garnet, and a yellow grossular, sometimes known as hyacinth, can be mistaken for a golden topaz.

Golden-amber is a *spessartite*; orange to russet is a *hessonite*; and deep pink to raspberry red is the popular *rhodolite*, named after the flowering rhododendron. Additional stones from the garnet family include: *almandine*, found in black or deep red with a violet tint; *pyrope,* found in red with a brownish tint or sometimes black; and the emerald green *uvarovite*.

The garnet has been traced back to ancient times and has a rich legacy of folklore. The gemstone was believed to soothe discord and promote peace; it also symbolized love, fidelity, truth, and passion, and the wearer was considered to be loyal, friendly, and energetic. Garnets were thought to control the loss of blood and cure diseases. These gems were believed to protect travelers, which could explain the garnet necklaces found adorning

Egyptian mummies on their journeys into the afterlife.

During the Victorian Era, a garnet was known as a *carbuncle*. The stone's popularity was enhanced by the creator of Sherlock Holmes, Sir Arthur Conan Doyle, who wrote The Adventure of the Blue Carbuncle around the turn of the last century. The carbuncle in this Holmes' mystery was, in fact, a garnet, which is found in almost every color *except* blue. Conan Doyle, most likely aware of this fact, could have decided on the stone's color precisely for this reason.

Dreaming of a garnet has been interpreted to mean that solving a problem is imminent. Another interpretation is that such a dream symbolizes great wealth. And possessing the stone will ensure that the owner's house is protected from lightning.

The garnet is a premier gem! The potential buyer is offered an array of colors, shapes, and sizes. These stones require little maintenance, adding to their popularity in gemstone jewelry pieces.

IOLITE

COLOR: various shades of blue to violet
MOHS' HARDNESS: 7 - 7.5

When placed at different angles and in different lighting, iolite reveals subtle shades of deep blue, grayish blue, and violet. The intriguing iolite received its name from the Greek words *ion*, meaning violet and *lithos*, meaning stone.

This gem is clean, crisp, and brilliant and may resemble

the regal sapphire, although an iolite is not as durable. Nevertheless, it is often called the **water sapphire**.

Iolite is also known as the *stone of friendship*. As this unique gem becomes more abundant, it increases in popularity for use in jewelry pieces. Iolite is either faceted or cabochon cut for use in rings, earrings, pendants, bracelets, pins, and necklaces.

One legend relates that, using iolite's light-absorption quality, the Vikings were able to determine the sun's location on overcast days, enabling them to navigate on the open seas.

Iolite requires only normal care and maintenance. Simply clean this gemstone with a soft, dry cloth.

JADE

COLOR: various shades of green, white, gray, red-orange, and yellow
MOHS' HARDNESS: 6 - 7

Jade is one of the older known gems, dating back to prehistoric times when it was used for weapons, utensils, and other implements. The stone has been found in ruins throughout Central and South America, Mexico, and China. For several thousand years, the Chinese as well as the Japanese have venerated jade, which was also prized by Central and South American Indians who considered it far more valuable than gold. The complex art of jade carving ended in America with the advent of Columbus. In China, however, the art has never been interrupted and continues today.

In fact, for thousands of years, the Chinese culture centered around jade. In earlier times, the Chinese considered this **stone of heaven**, as they called it, a symbol of high rank and authority, since only aristocrats and nobility could afford it.

To this day, jade remains the most popular gem throughout the Orient and, because it symbolizes love, it is an important part of Chinese wedding ceremonies. A toast to wish the bride and groom good fortune is: "May your hall be filled with jade and gold."

The stone is also popular in India where it is carved into small buddhas. To rub a buddha's belly is considered good luck, as is wearing any jade jewelry. Wearing jade is also believed to prevent harm, inspire bravery, and ensure prosperity, good health, and long life. In Central and South America, in pre-Columbian times, jade was ground into powder and ingested to cure kidney ailments.

This versatile stone is ideal for use in brooches, rings, pendants, earrings, necklaces, bracelets, and cufflinks as well as in ornamental and religious objects. The Chinese believe the more you wear jade, the more it becomes a part of you and, in its own way, "adopts" you. Jade symbolizes strength, harmony, and intelligence, and jade beads symbolize friendship, while talismans bring good luck to jockeys.

Be careful when buying this gemstone, for it has long been copied and altered. Inferior jade is often dyed and sold at inflated prices. In fact, eighty percent of the jade in today's marketplace is dyed or enhanced. You should also be aware that, while aventurine, serpentine, and chrysoprase are beautiful green stones, they are *not* jade.

Although genuine jade is easy to maintain, the gem is somewhat porous; therefore, most commercial jewelry cleaners should not be used. Simply clean it with a dry cloth, and either hang jade beads or lay them flat on a soft cloth.

Jadeite

COLOR: various shades of brown, green, orange, violet, white, yellow, and spotted black
MOHS' HARDNESS: 6.5 - 7

The jade family includes *jadeite* and **nephrite**, with jadeite being more durable as well as more desirable and costly. Jadeite is found in almost every color and, with the exception of green, colored jadeite is pale and unevenly textured. The most coveted and expensive is the rich emerald green *Imperial Jadeite*, frequently called *Imperial Jade.* Today, jadeite is classified among the world's leading gemstones. For the last several centuries, it has been found only in Burma in its natural state.

Nephrite

COLOR: various shades of brown, white, green, and spotted black
MOHS' HARDNESS: 6 - 6.5

Nephrite is the old, original Chinese jade with a more limited color range. This gem is popular in many countries including the United States. Much more common than jadeite, nephrite is naturally less expensive, with some commercial sources today being Wyoming, Alaska, and China. While it resembles jadeite, nephrite is slightly softer, although both are durable stones.

JASPER

COLOR: various colors and almost always
striped or spotted
MOHS' HARDNESS: 6.5 - 7

Jasper, a chalcedony in the quartz family, is available in almost every color and pattern imaginable and is rarely found in one solid color. The stone is easily recognized by its combination of spots and stripes of contrasting colors, the most popular of which is red and green. The color variations, together with the spots and stripes, enhance the beauty of jasper and result in its frequent use in fashion jewelry as well as ornamental objects and mosaics.

This stone dates back to ancient civilizations and, in the days of the Pharaohs, was highly regarded as an amulet believed to protect the heart. In early Christianity, jasper was recognized as St. Peter's foundation stone. Later, the gem was believed capable of bringing rain and driving away evil spirits. According to the most widespread and persistent legend, jasper had the power to cure a victim of poisonous snake bites.

Jasper is hard and durable and requires little care or maintenance; simply clean it with a soft, dry cloth.

KUNZITE

COLOR: various shades of pink and violet
MOHS' HARDNESS: 6 - 7

Kunzite has rapidly become one of the more popular gems in the spodumene family. Noted gemologist George F. Kunz introduced this brilliant stone, which bears his name, to the gem world nearly a century ago. Whether set in gold or silver, kunzite is an excellent choice for use in jewelry pieces because of its subtle pink shades and because the stone is readily available in larger sizes, which are moderate in cost.

Since kunzite has recently been added to the gem family, no folklore or legends have evolved from this stone; however, it does have a strange and unique characteristic, which would inspire superstition and mystery. That is, this gem has the unique ability to absorb sunlight or artificial light and emit that light in the dark; consequently, kunzite is often referred to as *the evening stone*.

Although relatively hard, this stone is brittle and may easily be chipped as the result of a sharp blow. Therefore, protective settings are recommended for kunzite jewelry, especially rings. You should also be aware that this gemstone's color may fade and lose some of its brilliance. While kunzite requires only normal care and maintenance, remember to handle it gently.

LAPIS LAZULI

COLOR: blue
MOHS' HARDNESS: 6

From the Arabic word *lazuli* meaning blue and the Latin word *lapis* meaning stone, lapis lazuli is an azure to deep blue opaque gem. Most of the world's supply of quality lapis, which is quite costly, is mined in the Hindu Kush region of Afghanistan. The gem may be speckled with white or gold pyrite inclusions and is often cabochon cut for rings, pendants, and other jewelry pieces. Lapis beads, the height of today's fashion, are often interspersed with pearls and/or gold beads to create a rich contrast.

This gemstone, dating back to the Babylonian and Egyptian Empires, was highly regarded then as it is today. To ensure they could see in the next world, ancient Egyptians laid stones of lapis on the eyes of mummies. A world famous Egyptian collection, in the Boston Museum of Fine Arts, includes ancient lapis lazuli.

For thousands of years, lapis was said to have great power and has symbolized success and divine favor. Worn as an amulet, the stone was believed to ward off illness and evil spirits.

Women of nobility used a form of lapis as make-up, and medieval painters ground and mixed it for ultramarine color pigmentation, the results of which can be seen in some of the world's famous paintings.

Lapis was also used to remedy eye ailments, relieve anxiety, and treat asthma. In addition, the gem has been found imbedded in ancient castle walls, weapons of war, and mosaics. Vases and other ornaments carved from lapis have also been found.

Be aware that sodalite, dyed agate, and other gems are often mistaken, and used as substitutes, for the more expensive and rarer lapis. One extreme way to identify lapis is by placing a small drop of hydrochloric acid on the stone. Genuine lapis lazuli containing pyrite will immediately emit a rotten egg odor. But a simpler way to determine if lapis has been dyed, or if another stone has been dyed to resemble lapis, is by moistening a cloth or paper towel with nail polish remover. Rub a small, unobtrusive part of the gem with the cloth and, if a stone has been dyed, the blue color will come off.

Only normal care and cleaning is required for this dramatic gemstone; simply clean it with a soft, dry cloth.

MALACHITE

COLOR: various shades of green
MOHS' HARDNESS: 3.5 - 4

Malachite, a copper ore, has been popular through the centuries because of its unique coloration that includes bands of contrasting shades of green. Although the stone polishes well, malachite is too soft for faceting; however, this softness lends itself to cabochon cuts for use in beads, bracelets, pins, and pendants as well as for carving objects of art such as statues.

Malachite has long been recognized as *a friendly stone.* According to legend, placing this stone on the stomach of a woman in labor would ensure an easy birth. The gem was also thought to cure eye diseases, protect its wearer from the evil eye, and guarantee good fortune. In addition, wearing malachite charms ensured sound sleep.

Ancient Egyptians used malachite for ornamentation, amulets, and powder for eye shadow. The Greeks and, later, the Romans copied these creations. In the Middle Ages, the gemstone was said to protect against witches and, especially, against dangers to children.

Be advised that any product containing ammonia could destroy this gemstone's striking beauty. Malachite requires only normal care and maintenance; simply clean it with a soft, dry cloth.

MARCASITE

COLOR: glittering with brassy-colored luster
MOHS' HARDNESS: 6 - 6.5

Marcasite holds an unusual place in the world of jewelry, since it is not a gemstone. Although classified as a mineral, **genuine** marcasite is unsuitable for jewelry since, when exposed to air, it will readily turn to powder. The "marcasite" used for jewelry pieces is in fact pyrite, another brassy colored metallic mineral often called *fool's gold.*

For many centuries, "marcasite" has been used for jewelry as well as for small bowls and figurines. Fashion jewelry of "marcasite" has gained in popularity, and these pieces, found throughout the world, are relatively inexpensive. Additionally, "marcasite" is often found in old belt buckles and various other items and is highly regarded by antique dealers.

In ancient times, Aztec and Mayan Indians used pyrite, or what we call "marcasite," to fashion exquisite mirrors of the highest quality. Their priests and medicine men also wore amulets of this mineral, believing that it bestowed magical powers.

Because "marcasite" is brittle and will corrode when exposed to dampness, most commercial jewelry cleaners should not be used for your jewelry pieces. Exercise caution in the care and maintenance of "marcasite," and simply clean it with a soft polishing cloth.

MOONSTONE

COLOR: colorless, champagne, and milky bluish-
white
MOHS' HARDNESS: 6 - 6.5

Moonstone, a member of the feldspar family, is popular because of its glowing brilliance. Although favored mostly for use in rings, this translucent gemstone enjoys widespread use in various other jewelry pieces. A pearly blue-white variety is highly regarded but has become increasingly rare and, therefore, more costly. An exotic rainbow moonstone, mined in the mountains of India, is aglow with a spectrum of colors.

Moonstone has long enjoyed a multitude of positive symbolism. The stone could have been named as the result of a myth about a tiny white spot that appears in the gem as the new moon begins. The spot gradually moves toward the center and slowly enlarges until it takes on a full-moon shape in the middle of the stone.

In ancient times, moonstone amulets were worn to prevent epileptic seizures. And hanging the gems from fruit trees was believed to guarantee greater crop yields. The stone was also believed to arouse tender passion and enable young lovers to foretell their futures. To see the future, however, the moonstone had to be placed in the mouth while the moon was full. Today, the gem is considered a good luck piece and is favored as a wedding gift.

Glass imitations are available but are of poor quality. This gemstone requires little care or maintenance; simply polish it with a soft, dry cloth.

ONYX

COLOR: apricot, black, green, orange, red, reddish-orange, and cream to dark brown, often alternating with white bands
MOHS' HARDNESS: 6.5 - 7

Onyx, a member of the quartz family, is a layered mineral found in its natural state in various colors. The bands in onyx are straight and parallel, while the bands in agate, another quartz variety, are curved. Onyx is used extensively for carving cameos, intaglios, and various objects of art. You should be aware, however, that the black "onyx" used for jewelry is often chalcedony, a different variety of quartz dyed black.

Wearing onyx was believed to be an evil omen for lovers, result in broken friendships, and promote bad dreams and fitful sleep. According to one legend, premature birth would result, if a pregnant woman wore the stone. On a more positive note, however, some cultures believed that placing an onyx on the stomach of a woman in labor would reduce pain and ensure a safe delivery. In India, women wore onyx necklaces to cool the fires of passion.

Many religious symbols are carved from onyx because the stone is said to inspire devotion. The stone is also said to lend courage and fearlessness, and dreaming of onyx is believed to ensure a happy marriage. For centuries, in the United States as well as throughout Europe, onyx jewelry has been worn by those in mourning.

Onyx requires only minimal care and maintenance. Simply polish this fascinating gemstone with a soft, dry cloth.

OPAL

COLOR: various shades in the entire spectrum of
         colors
MOHS' HARDNESS: 5.5 - 6.5

The opal is a dramatic gemstone as a result of its dazzling and fiery *play of color* that flashes out like tiny rainbows. This natural phenomenon results from layered silica spheres, which the ancient Greeks and Romans believed to be small rubies, emeralds, amethysts, and other gemstones, within each opal.

These gems are categorized as *precious, fire,* and *common,* the finest and rarest of which are black precious opals. Physical properties vary in that the stones are either transparent, translucent, or opaque and many are iridescent. Formed millions of years ago, mineralized geodes are unearthed and cracked open to obtain dazzling opals. The stones are cut either flat or in cabochons, since additional brilliance would not be captured by faceting.

Ignorance, fear, and misunderstanding once led to unfairly labeling the opal as a stone of evil and misfortune that would bring its owner bad luck. As those early superstitions faded, positive symbolism and good omens evolved. In classical times, the opal became a symbol of fidelity and religious devotion.

This gemstone was also believed to have medicinal value and could strengthen the eyes and protect them from disease. In the Orient, precious opals represent loyalty and hope. Many cultures thought the stone embodied truth and innocence, while others used it as a crystal ball to foretell the future. Dreaming of opals is interpreted to mean that you will have great possessions in your life-time.

Opal is the October birthstone, most likely because of its brilliant and vibrant colors that resemble a fall foliage display. Opals were especially favored by England's Queen Victoria who bestowed opal jewelry on each of her five daughters when they married. And that famous nineteenth century actress Sarah Bernhardt never appeared in public without her trademark — opal jewelry.

When purchasing what Shakespeare called *the Queen of Gems*, pay close attention to the primary color and pattern and to the number and intensity of colors. The more brilliant the color, the more costly the opal. Ensure that your opals are in protective settings, since these gems are sensitive to pressure and hard knocks.

Be aware that opals are sometimes used in doublets and triplets, where thin pieces of brilliant opal are mounted on pieces of lesser quality or on stones such as onyx.

Also be aware that many imitations are produced, and synthetic stones are widely sold. But genuine opals require special attention, since they contain from 25 to 30% water and, without proper care, tend to dry and crack. Keep these gems away from anything that is potentially drying and do not expose them to sudden, extreme temperature changes. Occasionally, wipe them lightly with olive oil or water, but never soak them.

Read directions for commercial jewelry cleaners carefully; most solutions are **not** for use with opals. Also be cautious with make-up and other chemical-based substances, which could compromise the beauty of this stone.

PEARL

COLOR: black, blue, cream, gold, green, lavender,
        peach, pink, silver, and white
MOHS' HARDNESS: 3 - 4

Although the gems in this family can easily be confused, pearls are of two basic types: *natural* and *cultured*.

The *natural* pearl is produced by the nonedible variety of oyster in salt water and is one of the rarer gems. A natural pearl can also be produced by mussels or oysters in fresh water lakes and rivers. In either case, the process occurs when a small foreign particle, such as a grain of sand, finds its way into the shell and tissue of the mollusk. To ease the discomfort of the irritant and to protect its soft tissues, the mollusk produces several coatings of *nacre,* also known as mother-of-pearl. When many layers of nacre have built up, a pearl is formed.

The *cultured* pearl is much more plentiful and moderate in cost because, to assist nature, man inserts the irritant into the mollusk. Although producing fine cultured pearls takes years, they are, nevertheless, harvested much sooner than natural pearls of the same size. Fine cultured pearls are often more rounded than natural pearls, an important quality for fashioning strands of necklaces and bracelets.

Culturing mabé pearls originated in the Orient in the early 1900s. Because these salt water pearls are produced in oysters with flat backs, mabé pearls are rounded on one side and flat on the other.

As their name implies, freshwater pearls are cultured in fresh water. To produce these irregular-shaped gems, a piece of live mussel is inserted into another mussel to stimulate pearl growth.

Imitation pearls are manufactured from glass or plastic and are *entirely* artificial. The difference between imitation and genuine pearls can readily be seen when the two are placed side by side. The quality and value of a **genuine** pearl can be determined by examining its:

- ☑ shape
- ☑ luster
- ☑ color
- ☑ freedom from blemishes
- ☑ size

Natural pearls are weighed as grains, four grains equaling one carat, and sold according to weight. Cultured pearls are measured in millimeters and sold according to size.

Pearls are used for fashioning rings, earrings, pins, bracelets, and pendants, often enhanced with diamonds, emeralds, or a variety of other gemstones. But a strand of pearls, whether natural or cultured, is a basic accessory for today's fashions, from shimmering evening gowns to conservative business suits. A long strand of cream or white pearls is stunning when twisted together with a strand of pink, peach, or lavender. A deep green malachite or rich blue lapis lazuli necklace worn together with a stark-white strand of pearls commands attention. And a ruby, amethyst, or sapphire slide suspended from a pearl strand provides much excitement.

Today's pearl trade centers in the Orient. Ninety percent of the pearls on the market are cultured, and seventy percent of all pearls harvested are fashioned into strands. The largest pearl ever found weighs 450 carats and is displayed in a London museum.

Pearls were used for adornment five to seven thousand years ago. In antiquity, our ancestors believed that pearls were produced when open oysters caught dew drops, said to be divine tears, that fell into the sea. Ancient Chinese thought the gems formed in dragon brains.

Caring for pearls is important to their preservation. Remember they are delicate and brittle but, since they are also compact, they will not be damaged if you care for them properly. Pearls are sensitive to perspiration, cosmetics, hair spray and, surprisingly, to vinegar. Do not put pearls on until after you have dressed, applied make-up, used hair spray, and dabbed on perfume. After you take pearls off, wipe them with a damp cloth. However, under the best of conditions and even with the utmost care, a pearl's life span is usually between 100 and 150 years, more than a lifetime (for most) — but not forever.

Pearls **must** be worn frequently. If stored in a dark place such as a box or drawer, for extended periods of time, pearls will crack. They must also be cleaned often, but read directions for jewelry cleaning solutions carefully. Although most of these are **not** to be used for pearls, commercial cleaners *only* for pearls are available.

Also be aware that certain chemicals and other abrasives could seriously compromise your lustrous pearls. In addition, remember that these gems are easily scratched and must be kept away from other jewelry. When not wearing your pearls, lay them flat on a soft cloth. To reduce the danger of one pearl scratching another, be sure the strands are knotted between each pearl, and try to have them restrung every other year.

PERIDOT

COLOR: from light yellow-green to deep olive
MOHS' HARDNESS: 6.5 - 7

Peridot, from the French word for gem, is often called *the evening emerald* and, like emeralds, quality stones are found along the Red Sea. During the Middle Ages, Crusaders brought the peridot to Europe where it was often used in religious ceremonies and included in many European cathedral treasuries.

Because peridot has long been a symbol of the sun, these stones were almost always set in yellow gold. In this way, the gem could exert its full power against *terrors of the night.* Today, peridot is also set in white gold as well as silver and is used for fashioning elegant jewelry such as rings, earrings, and bracelets.

This sparkling gemstone was also thought to ensure a happy marriage, cure liver disease, and protect its wearer from nightmares and the evil eye. To expel evil and envious thoughts, the ancients meditated by using peridot as a focal point.

The largest cut peridot, weighing 310 carats, is on display at the Smithsonian Institution in Washington, D.C. Several other specimens of this brilliant gem may be seen at the American Museum of Natural History in New York.

In recent years, quality stones have become more costly, since peridot is not as readily available as it once was,

56

especially in larger sizes. When buying peridot jewelry, select protective settings for the stones, which are not exceedingly hard. In addition, because these gems are chemical-sensitive, remove jewelry pieces before applying make-up. Handle peridot with care, and clean these gemstones with a soft, dry cloth.

QUARTZ

COLOR: various shades of many colors; also colorless
MOHS' HARDNESS: 7

The quartz family is the most versatile in the gem world and encompasses a greater variety and larger number of gems than any mineral family. Quartz is enjoyed in a wide range of striking colors in stones that are transparent, translucent, or opaque. These gems are fairly durable and moderate in cost.

An ancient stone, quartz was believed to have started the first fire after the sun's rays reflected through it. In classical times, the Greeks believed quartz to be a healing stone and used quartz amulets to calm their minds.

Some of the more popular gemstones from the colorful quartz family are: agate, amethyst, aventurine, bloodstone, carnelian, chalcedony, citrine, jasper, onyx, rose quartz, and smoky quartz.

Rose Quartz

COLOR: pale to dark rose
MOHS' HARDNESS: 7

Over the years, rose quartz has been in great demand for

use in carving figurines, various other objects of art, lamp bases, and ashtrays. The stone also enjoys widespread use in necklaces and bracelets of quartz beads or chips and other jewelry such as pins, brooches, and earrings, for which it is usually cabochon cut. Rose quartz is also a good choice for fashion jewelry. At one time, the gem was moderate in cost but, in recent years, prices have increased slightly, especially for the deeper pink stones.

Because it tends to crack when dropped or when subjected to a strong blow, rose quartz requires careful handling. Otherwise, the gem requires little or no maintenance; simply clean it with a soft cloth.

Smoky Quartz

COLOR: smoky yellow to dark brown
MOHS' HARDNESS: 7

Named for its rich yellow to deep brown colors, smoky quartz is often mistaken for smoky topaz. This gem is found worldwide and is moderately priced. In recent years, smoky quartz has gained in popularity for use in large brooches and dinner rings and various other jewelry pieces. The clearer the stone, however, the more expensive it will be.

Like rose quartz, smoky quartz requires little or no maintenance and needs only to be cleaned with a soft cloth.

RUBY

COLOR: pale to deep red
MOHS' HARDNESS: 9

Ruby, *the Lord of Gems*, is found in various shades of red and, like sapphire, is of the corundum family. Highly prized throughout the ages as a stone of virtue, the brilliant, lustrous ruby is one of the rarer as well as one of the more durable gemstones, ranking second only to a diamond in hardness. In fact, certain rubies are more valuable than some diamonds of equal size.

These gemstones are either faceted or cabochon cut for luxurious jewelry pieces. After being cabochon cut, some stones reveal a six-sided star effect and are termed *star rubies*. These are highly regarded as are the deep purplish-red rubies known as *pigeon's blood*.

Rubies were thought to ensure a peaceful life and, in ancient times, Arabs believed that dreaming of rubies meant good fortune and good health. In India, darker rubies were thought to be *male* stones while those of lighter hues were considered *female*.

In medieval times, the ruby was a symbol of love and passion and ensured beauty to its owner. Additionally, owning a quality ruby set in a ring or brooch, and worn on the left side, assured peace with all men and the preservation of home and property.

Since the 15th century, the finest of these gems have been mined in Burma. Some of the newer synthetic rubies appear so natural that many are mistaken for genuine. To differentiate between a natural and a synthetic stone, remember that inclusions are common in genuine rubies.

Because of a ruby's hardness, the stone requires only normal care and cleaning. These gems may be cleaned with commercial jewelry solutions, including ultrasonic cleaners, which may be used safely for **rubies**, diamonds, and sapphires — **red**, white, and blue!

SAPPHIRE

COLOR: various shades of every color except red;
also colorless
MOHS' HARDNESS: 9

Sapphire is best known for its brilliance, hardness, and durability and for its various shades of blue, although it is found in many other colors. Because of the stone's availability, a sapphire is more affordable than a ruby, the only other gem in the corundum family. The rich blue *Ceylon Sapphire* is in great demand worldwide because of its clarity and rich blue color saturation. Both yellow and blue colored stones from hard rock mines in Montana are some of the many other beautiful sapphires. Because of their resemblance to diamonds, small, often called white, sapphires are used frequently as accents for a variety of gemstones.

Through the centuries, this stone has been the jewel of choice for popes as well as kings and other nobility. In fact, sapphire is considered **the Regal Gem** because many kings, believing the stones defended them from harm, wore sapphires as talismans.

Larger sapphires are rare and have been romanticized through their exotic names such as the **Star of India**. On display in New York's Museum of Natural History, this gemstone weighs 543 carats and is considered the largest cut *star sapphire* in the world. Three immense sapphires, weighing approximately 2,000 carats apiece, have been carved to outline the heads of three American presidents: Washington, Lincoln, and Eisenhower.

According to a Persian legend, the earth is held by a sapphire, and its color reflects in the sky. In ancient times, sapphires were considered to be a cure for poisoning. Ancient Etruscans coveted the sapphire as did European royalty throughout the Middle Ages, even though they believed blue sapphires to be lapis lazuli. The stone was thought to protect its wearer from harm, remove impurities from the body, and act as a cure all.

One belief, even today, is that a sapphire will remain loyal to its original owner and will continue to protect her or him, even if the stone transfers to the possession of another. The gem is further believed to promote fidelity and, if a woman is unfaithful, her sapphire will dim. In addition, this stone is said to provide strength, comfort, and courage and to calm anger.

Although a diamond has become the traditional stone of engagement in the United States, in England and in the United Kingdom, it is the regal blue sapphire.

In recent years, synthetic sapphires of gem quality have been available. Genuine sapphires are hard and durable, requiring only normal care and maintenance. Most commercial jewelry solutions may be used, and ultrasonic cleaners may be used safely for rubies, diamonds, and **sapphires** — red, white, and **blue**!

SCAPOLITE

COLOR: various shades of pink, violet, and yellow;
         also colorless
MOHS' HARDNESS: 5 - 6.5

Scapolite, from the Latin word *scapus* meaning stalk and the Greek word *lithos* meaning stone, had not been available in the marketplace for nearly half a century. Fortunately, this interesting gem was recently rediscovered in Africa and South America.

A durable gemstone, scapolite is available in various soft colors, with yellow being quite popular. In fact, when yellow scapolite is faceted or cabochon cut for jewelry, this gem is most appealing. The stone is fast becoming a favorite with collectors as well as with lovers of gemstone jewelry and, if the cost remains moderate, it may be seen more often in jewelry pieces.

Although scapolite is not an especially hard gem, it requires little care or maintenance.

SERPENTINE

COLOR: various shades of green, often banded
MOHS' HARDNESS: 2 - 5

From the Latin word *serpens* meaning serpent, this gemstone was named for its shiny, snake-like bands of green color. Serpentine varies in hardness from soft to semihard and is frequently mistaken for jade. In fact, the resemblance is often so close that it is sometimes misrepresented as the more costly and valuable green jade.

This appealing stone is used for wall and table inlay and objects of art and, more and more, for jewelry. Serpentine is readily available and moderate in cost.

In ancient times, serpentine was highly regarded as an amulet and protected the wearer from snake or other poisonous reptile bites. For the amulet to be effective, however, the stone had to be in its natural state.

When wearing serpentine jewelry, be aware that this stone is quite soft and not especially durable. Clean serpentine carefully with a soft, dry cloth.

SODALITE

COLOR: various shades of blue and gray
MOHS' HARDNESS: 5.5 - 6

Named because of its sodium content, sodalite has been recognized as such for less than two hundred years. All shades of blue are at least somewhat interspersed with white streaks. This gem is often used for fashioning rings, pins, and earrings as well as beaded necklaces and bracelets. Sodalite jewelry complements many of today's fashions, especially blue denim. The stone is also widely used in crafting various objects of art.

Despite its relatively short existence in the marketplace, sodalite is recognized as the gem of Canada. Although no folklore has evolved from this stone, many scarabs for contemporary jewelry are carved from sodalite. In ancient Egypt a scarab was a sacred amulet, symbolizing the sun and resurrection.

Be aware that some sodalite closely resembles the more costly lapis lazuli. Most commercial jewelry cleaners should not be used for sodalite; simply clean it with a soft, dry cloth.

SPINEL

COLOR: various shades of almost every color
MOHS' HARDNESS: 8

Spinel is a dazzling gem found in a variety of colors, the most popular of which is the clear *ruby spinel*. This stone was recognized as a separate gem only about two centuries ago. Until then, spinels were thought to be rubies and sapphires, even though they had more brilliance than either. Unfortunately, even after spinel was granted its own identity, it was not widely recognized for its beauty. But the gem is gaining in popularity because of its radiance and moderate price.

Two of the larger spinels ever discovered are now part of the British Crown Jewels and, although uncut, both have been polished. Many fine spinels can also be found in the treasuries of Iran and Russia, and a dark red spinel, weighing 398 carats, is incorporated in the Czar's Crown. But larger stones, especially of this size, are rare.

In ancient times, because of its rarity and brilliance, the red spinel, although thought to be a ruby, was considered a potent medicine for curing infections and inflammations. This gem was also believed to calm the spirit.

Synthetic spinels, which number approximately 200, are of good quality and are highly regarded. In fact, genuine spinels are often mistaken for synthetic versions.

Spinel is a durable gemstone, requiring little care or maintenance.

TANZANITE

COLOR: various shades of blue and violet
MOHS' HARDNESS: 6.5 - 7

Tanzanite, a transparent variety of zoisite, was named by Tiffany & Company when it was discovered in the mid-1960s. While this gemstone is mined only in Tanzania, dull-brown zoisite can be heat-treated to become brilliant tanzanite, from the richest cobalt blue to deep bluish-purple.

In the 1990s, jewelry lovers and collectors became enthralled with this dazzling gem. Within a short time, however, the supply of tanzanite has been seriously depleted. While smaller stones remain moderate in price, larger tanzanites are quite costly.

Although tanzanite jewelry has become popular, remember that this stone is fragile. These striking gems must be mounted in protective settings and, even then, be careful when wearing tanzanite pieces, especially rings.

Also be careful when cleaning and storing this dramatic gemstone, and be aware that good glass imitations are available on the open market.

TOPAZ

COLOR: various shades of blue, green, pink,
        red-orange, violet, and yellow; also colorless
MOHS' HARDNESS: 8

Topaz, a brilliant and versatile gem, is found in various shades of many colors. The most available stones are those in shades of blue, commonly referred to as **Sky**

Blue, Swiss Blue, and **London Blue**. Sky Blue is the palest, while London Blue is the richest and deepest in color and the most expensive of the three. Many topaz stones receive their coloration by heat-treating colorless topaz, but some of the blue and various other colors are found in their natural states.

The readily available colored stones and the colorless, often called white topaz, are usually faceted and set in jewelry pieces, such as rings, bracelets, pendants, and earrings. Smaller white topaz stones are excellent for accenting blue topaz, citrine, peridot, amethyst, garnet, and a variety of other gems.

Blue topaz, along with white, is the most popular and moderate in cost; however, the gold-colored stone holds a place of prominence in the topaz family, with the deep red-orange **Imperial Topaz** being considered the finest. To enhance its beauty and its rich color, an Imperial Topaz is often accented with small diamonds.

The topaz has long been recognized as a symbol of love and affection. In classical times, the gem was considered a stone of strength that could calm the mind, body, and spirit. During the Middle Ages, powdered topaz was used for medicinal purposes and was especially regarded as a cure for asthma, insomnia, burns, hemorrhages, and vision impairments. In fact, in the 12th century, Saint Hildegaard reportedly cured a patient's dim vision by using a lotion into which she had placed a topaz.

No adverse legends are associated with this gemstone, once believed to bestow good health on its wearer. In the past, and even today, topaz symbolizes friendship, integrity, faithfulness, and goodness.

Remove topaz jewelry before applying make-up, and keep

these stones away from chemicals, especially sulfuric acid. Otherwise, topaz requires only normal care and maintenance.

TOURMALINE

COLOR: multicolored and various shades of
almost every color; also colorless
MOHS' HARDNESS: 7 - 7.5

We learn more every year about the almost endless varieties of tourmaline, classified as such by gemologists only since the 18th century. Although not identified by its contemporary name, the stone was known during the classical period throughout the Mediterranean.

Few gemstones are found in as wide a variety of rich colors as the tourmaline. Some of these gems are readily available and affordable even in larger sizes; however, others are not as abundant and are quite costly. Tourmalines are durable stones that are either faceted or cabochon cut for jewelry pieces such as rings, earrings, pins, and pendants. They are also carved or fashioned into beads for bracelets and necklaces.

The colorless variety of tourmaline is known as *achroite*, which is rare. A yellow to dark brown stone is a *dravite*; more common shades of green are *verdelites*; shades of blue, not readily available, are *indicolites*; and brilliant pink to red shades are *rubellites*. Another popular type is the *watermelon* tourmaline that looks, not surprisingly, like a cross section of watermelon.

Because of the many color variations, tourmalines may easily be confused with a multitude of other gems as well as with glass imitations. But the versatile tourmaline requires only normal care and maintenance.

TURQUOISE

COLOR: various shades of blue, green, and blue-green
MOHS' HARDNESS: 5 - 6

Called *the lucky stone* by the Turks, turquoise dates back at least seven thousand years, having been recovered from Egyptian tombs. The stone was so named because, for many years, it was brought from Asia to Europe through *Turkey*. Most turquoise includes brown, gray, or black veins that enhance this already beautiful stone. However, the finest pieces of pure robin egg blue, which are both rare and valuable and often set in gold, have no veins.

Turquoise is usually cabochon cut for use in rings, bracelets, pendants, earrings, and amulets. The stone is also carved into religious ornaments and beads, tumbled for bracelets and necklaces, and polished in thin strips for inlay work.

Turquoise is highly prized throughout Asia and Africa not only for its beauty but also for its healing qualities. Because the gem has been known as turquoise since antiquity, the folklore is extensive and, at times, contradictory.

According to legend, the gem protected its wearer from poison, reptile bites, eye diseases, and the evil eye. The stone was also thought capable of predicting impending death. Furthermore, it was believed that bladder ailments were cured by drinking water in which a turquoise had been dipped. One legend relates that this gemstone enabled Buddha to destroy a monster.

A belief even today is that, if a turquoise glows brightly, its wearer is healthy but, if dull, the wearer is either ill or in poor spirits. And when the stone is colorless, it is drained of energy and useless to the owner. The gemstone is also believed to symbolize courage, success, and love.

For centuries, Southwest American Indians used turquoise as a form of currency. They also believed it would bring spoils to the warrior, animals to the hunter, and good luck to all. Furthermore, the gemstone was their primary holy stone, and each Navaho carried a personal turquoise piece. According to an Apache legend, a courageous warrior found turquoise by following a rainbow to its end and digging there in the moist earth.

Fashioning and selling turquoise jewelry, almost always set in silver, is a major source of income today for Southwest American Indians. And Mexican Aztecs often use the stone in their exquisite mosaic pieces.

Because this superb gemstone is frequently simulated, a potential buyer must be careful. Glass imitations are difficult to distinguish from genuine turquoise. In addition, various stones are sometimes dyed. To determine if a stone has been dyed to resemble turquoise, moisten a cloth with nail polish remover, and rub a small, unobtrusive part of the gem. Any dye will come off on the cloth.

Be aware that this gemstone is porous, and the stone's color may be damaged by light, perspiration, oils, and cosmetics. When possible, remove turquoise rings before washing your hands. And since these stones are relatively soft and easily scratched, they should be in protective settings and stored separately from other jewelry. Most commercial jewelry cleaners should not be used for turquoise; simply clean it with a soft, dry cloth.

ZIRCON

COLOR: various shades of blue, brown, green,
orange, red, and yellow; also colorless
MOHS' HARDNESS: 6.5 - 7.5

Zircon, found in a variety of colors, is one of the few natural gemstones approaching the dispersive quality of a diamond. Colorless and blue zircons usually result from heat treatment; green are the most rare. While this brilliant gem has enjoyed a splendid past, the zircon is not in abundance today, and the cost has greatly increased. When available, however, these transparent gemstones are used to fashion elegant jewelry pieces such as rings, earrings, pendants, and necklaces.

Carved zircons have been found in ancient archeological sites. The stone is mentioned in biblical passages, and early writings refer to it as *Jargoon, Hyacinth*, and *Jacinth.* In the Middle Ages, this gem was believed to have great powers, especially for men, and was thought to protect them from evil spirits, strengthen their bodies, and restore their appetites. In addition, zircon was said to induce sleep, ward off bad dreams, and banish grief and sadness. For women, the gemstone was said to assist in childbirth. And anyone wearing a zircon would not only be wealthy but also wise.

Be careful when wearing zircons because they are brittle and can be easily chipped or scratched. When used for jewelry pieces, especially rings, the stones must be mounted in protective settings. Keep zircons away from other jewelry pieces, and store them separately in soft pouches.

Extended exposure to direct sunlight could alter this gem's

color. Also be aware that blue zircons have been reported to fade when worn in tanning booths. And one final note. Do not confuse this natural gemstone with manmade cubic zirconia.

THE MAGIC OF COLOR

Gemstone jewelry has been the most prized adornment of all mankind, and its dazzling beauty lies in the magic of its color. The luster of the precious metal in which a gemstone is set, the elegance of the cut, and the decorative style of the setting complement a gem but, in the final analysis, the intriguing charm and brilliance of a stone's color create a passion that never subsides. One never tires of admiring that special gemstone piece or, for that matter, all the pieces one may be fortunate enough to own.

In ancient times, gems represented wealth and power. As time passed, gemstones were highly regarded as cures for ailments and diseases. Later, gem colors were believed to have supernatural powers and religious connotations and symbolized individual strengths and weaknesses, some of which are:

❖ RED
   for a man, nobility; for a woman, pride
❖ WHITE (COLORLESS)
   for a man, integrity; for a woman, purity
❖ BLUE
   for a man, wisdom; for a woman, vigilance
❖ YELLOW
   for a man, secrecy; for a woman, generosity

❖ GREEN

for a man, joy; for a woman, ambition

❖ VIOLET

for a man, solemnity; for a woman, spiritual love

And the magic of color in gems continues. The number of hues and shades is almost beyond comprehension and, although we purchase gemstones for the beauty of their colors, many individuals reflect on the mystique, which lies beyond the magical colors that so enthrall us.

... the intriguing charm and brilliance of a stone's color ....

GEMS AND THEIR SYMBOLISM

Gems and their symbolism have intrigued mankind for thousands of years. History has revealed that gems were believed to have mystical powers and that they controlled individuals as well as empires. These dazzling stones brought fortune or misfortune and were used to cure illness and bestow virtue.

Inevitably, this mystique led one to assume that gemstones had supernatural powers. Gems became inexorably linked to the sun, the moon, and other celestial bodies. This astrological connection, which introduced gems into religion, became a driving force from the cradle to the grave.

Through the centuries, some gems were designated as birthstones, according to months of the year. Myths as well as symbolic virtues, such as courage, fidelity, and hope, gradually evolved from these stones. Many wear stones associated with their birthdays to ensure good luck. The following chart lists birthstone designations:

GEMS BY BIRTH MONTH

Month	Traditional Stone	Alternate
January	Garnet (constancy)	
February	Amethyst (sincerity)	
March	Aquamarine (courage)	Bloodstone Jasper
April	Diamond (innocence)	White Topaz Rock Crystal
May	Emerald (love, success)	Chrysoprase
June	Pearl (health, longevity)	Alexandrite Moonstone Agate

GEMS BY BIRTH MONTH (Continued)

Month	Traditional Stone	Alternate
July	**Ruby** (contentment)	Carnelian
August	**Peridot** (happy marriage)	Sardonyx Jade
September	**Sapphire** (clear thinking)	Lapis Lazuli Blue Coral
October	**Opal** (hope)	Tourmaline Beryl
November	**Golden Topaz** (fidelity)	Citrine Amber
December	**Turquoise** (prosperity)	Blue Zircon Blue Topaz

Additionally, some gems were designated according to signs of the zodiac as follows:

GEMS BY ZODIAC SIGN

Aquarius	January 20 - February 18	Garnet
Pisces	February 19 - March 20	Amethyst
Aries	March 21 - April 19	Bloodstone
Taurus	April 20- May 20	Sapphire
Gemini	May 21 - June 20	Agate
Cancer	June 21 - July 22	Emerald

GEMS BY ZODIAC SIGN (Continued)

Leo	July 23 - August 22	Onyx
Virgo	August 23 - September 22	Carnelian
Libra	September 23 - October 22	Peridot
Scorpio	October 23 - November 21	Beryl
Sagittarius	November 22 - December 21	Topaz
Capricorn	December 22 - January 19	Ruby

Gemstones also continue to have a symbolic role in religion, and the following gems have been closely aligned with two of the world's major religions — Judaism and Christianity:

THE TWELVE TRIBES OF ISRAEL

Tribe	Stone
Levi	Garnet
Zebulon	Diamond
Gad	Amethyst
Benjamin	Jasper
Simeon	Peridot
Issachar	Sapphire
Naphtali	Agate
Joseph	Onyx
Reuben	Sard
Judah	Emerald
Dan	Topaz
Asher	Beryl

THE TWELVE APOSTLES

Apostle	Stone
Peter	Jasper
Andrew	Sapphire
James	Chalcedony
John	Emerald
Philip	Sardonyx
Bartholomew	Sard
Matthew	Peridot
Thomas	Beryl
James the Less	Topaz
Jude	Chrysoprase
Simon	Zircon
Judas	Amethyst

However, gemstone symbolism did not end there. Gemstones and certain precious metals became wedding anniversary symbols, which are popular even today, as follows:

WEDDING ANNIVERSARIES

First	Pink Beryl; Aquamarine
Second	Crystal
Third	Chrysoprase
Fourth	Moonstone
Fifth	Carnelian
Sixth	Peridot
Seventh	Coral
Eighth	Opal
Ninth	Citrine
Tenth	Turquoise
Eleventh	Garnet

WEDDING ANNIVERSARIES (Continued)

Twelfth	Amethyst
Thirteenth	Agate
Fourteenth	Ivory
Fifteenth	Topaz
Twentieth	Platinum
Twenty-fifth	Silver
Thirtieth	Pearl
Thirty-fifth	Jade
Fortieth	Ruby
Forty-fifth	Sapphire
Fiftieth	Gold
Fifty-fifth	Emerald
Sixtieth	Diamond

Much of the richness and impact of this symbolism, however, belongs to the past. Today, the hallmarks of a gemstone are its color, beauty, and value.

... a courageous warrior found turquoise by following a rainbow to its end and digging there in the moist earth....

JEWELRY AS ACCESSORIES

Throughout history, we have coveted gems and jewelry for various reasons. Today we wear jewelry primarily for its inherent beauty. Because jewelry manufacturing has become a multibillion dollar industry worldwide, our choices are overwhelming. But ultimately our selections are dictated by cost, style, and color preference, in both gems and precious metals.

The key role of jewelry has been its use as ornamental accessories, the ultimate in adornment being the royal crown. Over the centuries, kings and queens wore crowns enhanced with breathtakingly beautiful gemstones. Today, women adorn their heads with barrettes, hair combs, and even tiaras, especially for more formal occasions.

Earrings are worn extensively as accessories today and are of two basic types: clip-on and pierced. While thousands of women wear the pierced type, many men are having their ears pierced, the more popular choice being to pierce one ear only. And in some foreign cultures, a woman has the side of her nose pierced to insert a small gemstone.

Accessories for the neck can be found in a variety of styles. Necklaces and chokers fashioned from precious metals may consist of one or more chains. Pearl necklaces, and those of other gemstones such as quartz, jade, or jasper, may have one or more strands. When pearls and other gems used in strands are of the same size, they are called uniform; when they vary in size, they are called graduated. Some are worn close to the neck, while others hang loosely. They are connected by one of a multitude of fasteners, some of which are as ornamental as the piece itself. To further enhance the beauty of a chain or strand, a pendant, slide, charm, religious item, or locket may adorn the necklace.

Hand accessories are rings worn on fingers and, more and more, on thumbs. In ancient times, rings were worn on all the fingers, and this practice is gaining popularity today. Plain metal rings are often used to symbolize marriage; but many prefer wedding rings that have a table mounted with one or more gems. A ring with one stone is a solitaire; one with stones of uniform size encircling the band is an eternity ring, frequently symbolizing engagement or, more often, marriage. A ring with a crown that holds a large gem encircled by smaller ones is a cluster ring. Rings may also bear seals or insignias of lodges, associations, organizations, universities, military units, or religious orders.

Arm and leg ornaments are also popular accessories. In ancient times, bracelets and bangles worn on the upper arms were popular among nobility and the wealthy. Today, bracelets and bangles are worn on the wrists and/or lower arms, and bracelets, with or without gemstones, are worn on the ankles. These accessories can be found in a multitude of shapes, sizes, and patterns and are fastened by one of many types of clasps. A bangle may either be clasped or slipped over the hand. In many instances, charms and other small items are attached to bracelets.

Other jewelry worn as clothing, handbag, scarf, and hat accessories includes pins, brooches, belt buckles, cuff links, tie clasps, and tie tacks. And finally, gemstones and precious metals abound in watches and other time pieces.

GEMSTONE SETTINGS

You may consider various types of settings for your gemstones. Ultimately, your selection will be a matter of personal taste, but remember that the setting may well enhance the beauty of your gem(s) and, equally important, may protect the stone(s) from damage or loss. Also, regardless of the type of setting, remember to have your jewelry checked periodically for loose stones.

The illustrations that follow are but a few examples of the more popular ring settings; however, these are also used for other jewelry pieces such as bracelets, pendants, slides, earrings, brooches, and pins.

❖ PRONG SETTING

This setting has prongs, often four or six, that are tightened to hold the stone in place. Prong settings are the most widely used in rings and various other types of jewelry.

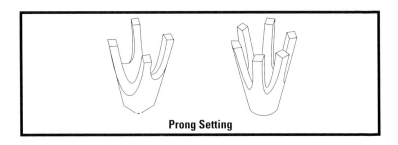

Prong Setting

❖ BEZEL SETTING

This setting has no prongs; instead a rim, or bezel, encompasses the stone and holds it in place. The bezel is molded to accommodate a specific stone.

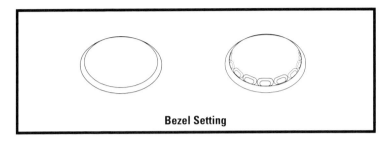

Bezel Setting

❖ CHANNEL SETTING

This setting is quite popular but more expensive because each stone must be precisely the same size and each must be hand set in the channel, which has no metal separations.

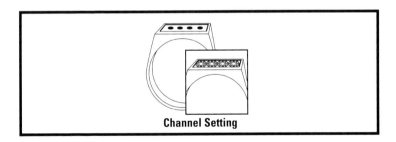

Channel Setting

❖ CLUSTER SETTING

This setting usually has one large stone and a number of smaller ones surrounding and complementing it, but it may also have any number of small stones arranged in a cluster.

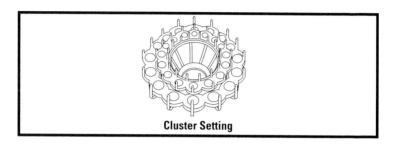

Cluster Setting

❖ PAVÉ SETTING

Many small stones are tightly clustered together in this setting where no metal shows through, giving the illusion that the jewelry piece, or part of it, is completely paved with stones.

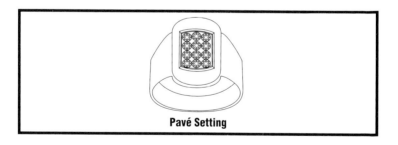

Pavé Setting

GEMSTONE SHAPES AND CUTS

The *shape* is sometimes confused with the *cut* of a stone. After color, the shape of a gemstone and especially its cut are important because they affect a stone's depth of color as well as its liveliness. A highly skilled lapidary cuts, shapes, and polishes gemstones and must ensure balance in each of the various shapes and precision in each of the cuts.

Shapes such as round, marquise, heart, or oval affect the overall appearance, or personality, of a stone and, to some extent, the personality of its owner. While selection of a *shape* is a matter of personal taste, a *well-cut* gemstone will retain its beauty and value indefinitely.

Cuts are of two basic types: *cabochon* and *faceted*, the older and simpler of these being the cabochon, often called dome-shaped. For a cabochon cut, the stone is smoothly rounded rather than faceted. Cabochon-cut stones are frequently shaped into ovals. A stone may also be faceted on the bottom and cabochon cut on the top.

The most common facet cut for a round shape is the brilliant. To facet for a brilliant cut, the top of the stone is ground flat into what is known as a table, from which the sides first slope outward, then inward. But various facet cuts are available for almost any stone shape.

The initial shaping and cutting of a stone determine whether it will be dull and listless or bright and beautiful. Some of the more popular gemstone shapes and cuts are as follows:

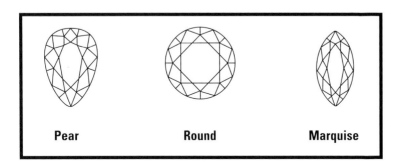

Pear   Round   Marquise

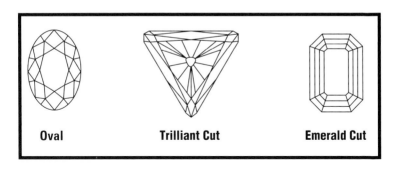

Oval   Trilliant Cut   Emerald Cut

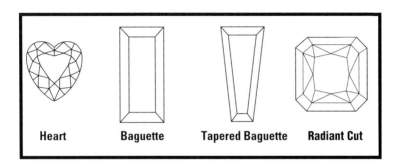

Heart   Baguette   Tapered Baguette   Radiant Cut

THE FOUR "C's"

Certain factors determine the value and quality of a gemstone, the most important of which are the following four "C's":

❖ COLOR

Color is considered the most important quality of a gemstone. While the number of hues and shades from which to choose are nearly unlimited, look for deep, rich coloration. Stay away from gems that are cloudy or opaque except, of course, in those such as opals. Above all, select stones that are pleasing to your own personal taste.

❖ CUT

Whether you choose a pear, oval, round, marquise, or any other shape, be especially aware of the cut, which must be balanced. You must remember that the cut determines depth of color and liveliness of the gem.

❖ CLARITY

While clarity is an important consideration, you must keep in mind that a completely flawless gem is rare. Consider inclusions, especially in a stone such as an emerald, as nature's way of adding variety, even to more costly stones.

❖ CARAT WEIGHT

The weight of a gemstone also determines the value of a quality stone. Most gems, except for those such as cultured pearls, are weighed in carats.

You must decide the importance of each individual "C" when purchasing your gemstone; then consider the gem by a collective evaluation of all four "C's." This will allow you to judge the beauty and durability of a stone, while choosing within your financial means.

While using the four "C's" is the accepted method of determining the value of a gemstone, the prospective buyer must also consider the following:

❖ DURABILITY
When purchasing a jewelry piece, especially one with a more fragile gemstone, think of when and where you will wear it. Make certain the setting will protect the stone. With proper care, most gemstones will last for centuries, if not forever.

❖ COLORATION
If your piece contains more than one gemstone, make certain that each stone matches in color.

❖ ZONING
Make certain the coloration of the gem is consistent throughout.

❖ RARITY
While the demand for gemstones is greater than ever, some stones are becoming more difficult to obtain, as supplies diminish.

CARE AND CLEANING

The main threat to the beauty and durability of fine jewelry is thoughtlessness, both in care and cleaning. Most jewelry is lost in public powder rooms when rings are removed, placed on a vanity, and forgotten; when pins and brooches are left on outer garments to be checked at public facilities or sent to the cleaners; or when jewelry pieces are not removed before the wearer participates in activities such as swimming.

Often jewelry is destroyed by sheer carelessness or neglect. While sturdy gold pieces require little in the way of cleaning and maintenance, certain gemstones must be treated gently and polished carefully. Pearls and amber pieces love to be worn or they will crack if tucked away in drawers and forgotten. And the more you wear sterling silver, the less it will tarnish.

A jewelry lover would be wise to purchase an armoire or simply a jewelry and/or ring box. Pieces of jewelry should be stored separately, either in lined compartments or in soft pouches, and must be kept away from humidity and temperature extremes. Whenever possible, remove jewelry before washing your hands or showering and also before applying make-up, deodorant, hair spray, hand lotion, and perfume. Never wear jewelry when participating in sports or other excessive activities, and always keep jewelry away from harmful chemicals and other abrasives.

The safest way to clean most jewelry is by immersing it in warm, sudsy water, then rinsing and drying it thoroughly or simply by wiping your pieces gently with a soft, dry cloth. Many department and jewelry stores sell polishing cloths that work well. Some cloths are for cleaning tarnish from silver and polishing it, and some are for cleaning and polishing gold.

A variety of commercial jewelry cleaners is available, and

many of these arc cxcellent. But always read directions carefully to ensure that the solution will not harm certain gemstones. Use ultrasonic cleaners **only** for rubies, diamonds, and sapphires. *Remember — red, white, and blue!* For cleaning other stones, refer to specific gem sections of this handbook.

Have a jeweler check your more expensive pieces regularly for loose prongs, bezels, and clasps. This would be a good opportunity to have the pieces professionally cleaned and polished as well.

CARAT OR KARAT?

Are you aware of the difference between *carat* and *karat* and how the terms apply to gemstones and gold? A carat is a measure of weight for gemstones, while a karat is a measure of gold quality by content.

In ancient times throughout the Mediterranean, fruit seeds from the carob, a type of evergreen, tree were used to weigh gems. A gemstone was placed on one side of a scale and carob seeds on the other, adding as many seeds as necessary to balance the scale. The word carat is likely a derivation of carob. Today, a carat (CT) is a measure of weight for gemstones, with one carat weighing one-fifth of a gram or two hundred milligrams. We also use a "point system" based on the premise that 100 points equal one carat. Therefore, a gem weighing 50 points is a half-carat stone; one weighing 75 points is three-quarters of a carat; a gem weighing 125 points is a one and a quarter-carat stone; and another weighing 150 points is a one and a half-carat gemstone.

The application of the word karat (K or KT) is slightly more complicated. The world standard for pure gold is set at 24 karats. Seldom is gold used in this whole or pure state because it is far too soft. For durability and color variance, gold is almost always alloyed with other metals such as silver or copper.

If a gold piece is 18K, it is three-quarters pure gold and one-quarter other metal(s); if 12K, it is one-half pure gold and one-half other metal(s). To be considered gold in the United States, a jewelry piece must be at least 10K; in Canada and England, at least 9K; and in France and Italy, at least 18K.

The more preferred karatage for gold in the United States is either 10, 14, or 18K, which is much more durable than high karat gold, that is, 20, 22, or 24K.

The following chart lists karatage and the corresponding percentage of pure gold content:

U.S. MARKS (GOLD)

Mark	Pure Gold Content
24K	100.0%
20K	83.0%
18K	75.0%
14K	58.3%
12K	50.0%
10K	41.7%

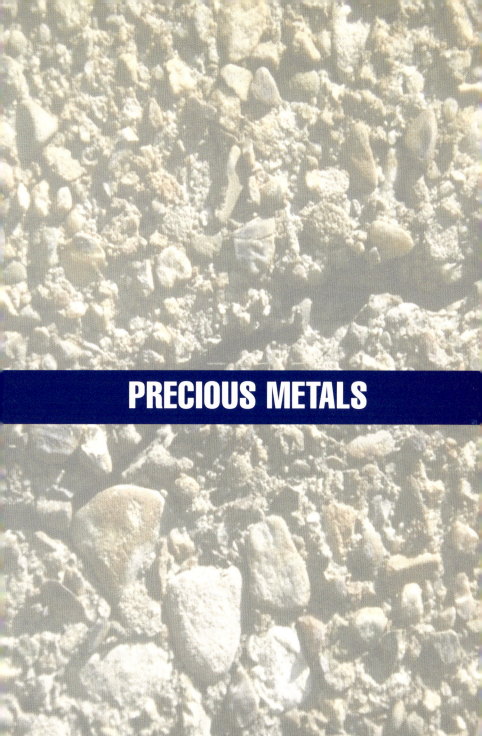

PRECIOUS METALS

GOLD

Gold has been, and remains to this day, the cornerstone of human development. The ultimate form of security and a symbol of wealth and power since at least 10,000 years ago, this precious metal has been closely associated with the sun and venerated as the source of life.

Ancient Egyptians believed the sun-god Ra, a principal deity, was ever-present in the form of large golden discs and other jewelry items. Egyptian nobility continued to be fascinated with gold throughout their lifetimes and required that gold items be entombed with them for all eternity.

The Egyptians found gold for their jewelry, coffins, and art objects in upper Egypt where, in the Eastern Desert between the Nile River and the Red Sea, gold mines were located. They mined for this, and other metals, with great success; however, all the gold in Egypt was considered the Pharaoh's property.

One legend from Greek mythology relates that Dionysus, the god of wine and vegetation, granted King Midas the power to turn everything he touched to gold. On the other side of the world, Peruvian Incas believed their kings to be of the sun-god family and adorned them as well as their palaces with massive amounts of shining gold.

Gold is the most malleable of all metals and, after silver, the most reflective. Because it will neither rust or corrode nor will its brightness fade, gold is considered *a noble metal.*

More than half of all the gold mined is used for jewelry and much of that is for the symbolic gold wedding band. Since gold is quite soft, however, it is rarely used in its pure state, which is 24 karat. For use in jewelry, gold is alloyed with other metals to strengthen it as well as to lighten its weight. Regardless of the alloys with which it is combined, the precise gold content, or karatage, is stamped on gold jewelry pieces. This is known as the karat mark, while the manufacturer's stamp is known as a hallmark.

Surprisingly, gold is quite rare and, after platinum, it is the most expensive of metals. Even though gold is every-where, on land and in water, it is not only difficult but also expensive to extract. An average of only *one ounce of gold* is extracted from *three tons of ore*. Despite its cost, how-ever, gold remains the most popular metal for use in jew-elry.

When purchasing gold jewelry, one has a number of col-ors from which to choose: yellow, white, rose, and green. Jewelry manufacturers mix pure gold with various combi-nations of alloys to achieve these colors and fashion stun-ning pieces. The countless choices in gold jewelry are simply a matter of personal taste.

SILVER

While not as valuable as gold or platinum, silver is the most reflective metal and, for many, it is preferred for jew-elry. For the most part, silver is mined in conjunction with lead, copper, and zinc ores and is a by-product of these various metals. After gold, it is the most malleable of all metals and must be mixed with alloys for hardness and durability.

Sterling silver used for jewelry is comprised of 92.5% silver and 7.5% other metals, often nickel. Because of the sulfur and sulfides in silver, the metal tarnishes easily, and frequent polishing is needed to maintain its lustrous shine.

Silver was used as legal tender in ancient civilizations several thousand years before Christ, and the shimmering metal symbolized wealth. Today, it is still coveted for its value and used for coins of various denominations.

Through the centuries, silver has been considered sacred in many religions and cults. Inca Indians described the metal as teardrops of the moon, and it was especially venerated by southwest American Indians and those in Central and South America as well.

During the Middle Ages, the metal was fashioned into jewelry, and silversmithing became a recognized craft. Silversmiths became proficient in creating eating and drinking vessels as well as objects of art. Until the nineteenth century when it was replaced by gold, silver was the universal monetary standard.

PLATINUM

Platinum, referred to as *the noblest of metals*, is more rare and more valuable than gold or silver. Although South America had been the main source for this noblest metal, three-fourths of the known reserves today are in southern Africa.

In the United States, platinum is identified by PT rather than K or KT and, in Europe, by 950 or PT950. Separating other platinum metals from platinum itself was not achieved until the early 19th century. Since then, this rich metal has been used for fashioning exquisite jewelry. Although its popularity decreased for a number of years, it has started to gain prominence, once again, in the jewelry world.

Because of its purity, platinum is favored by those who have allergies or reactions to other metals. But the price to be paid is that, while the grayish-white metal is pure and strong, it is also expensive and quite heavy.

Rhodium, another member of the platinum family, is even harder, more durable, and brighter than platinum and is often used to coat gold and even platinum jewelry. Rhodium coating will not wear off for many years and will either eliminate or, at least, help reduce allergic reactions to gold alloys. (For further information, see the section on allergies and other problems.) And rhodium is frequently used for diamond settings in rings and other fine jewelry pieces because its brightness enhances the brilliance of diamonds.

CHAINS AND CLASPS

As early as 2500 B.C., ancient artisans used narrow coils and chains of linked wire to make simple necklaces, bracelets, and earrings. Through the centuries, chain jewelry has increased in popularity with women and, because of the availability in different lengths, weights, and styles, many men enjoy wearing chains today.

The three precious metals, but mostly silver and gold are fashioned into chains for necklaces as well as wrist and ankle bracelets. Whether the chain is of yellow, rose, or white gold or whether it is of silver, various types of chain links are available. In fact, the variety is so extensive that selecting the *right* link for the *right* purpose can be difficult and confusing.

From an elegant herringbone to a simple, but sturdy, box link, chains have become jewelry essentials. They are worn either alone or with other chains or strands; they are worn with or without pendants or slides; and they are connected by one of various types of clasps.

To help you compare styles and to assist with your selections, some of the more popular chain links are pictured here.

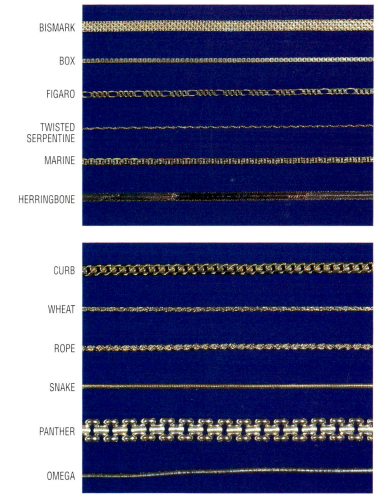

BISMARK

BOX

FIGARO

TWISTED SERPENTINE

MARINE

HERRINGBONE

CURB

WHEAT

ROPE

SNAKE

PANTHER

OMEGA

ALLERGIES AND OTHER PROBLEMS

Since pure gold is too soft for most jewelry, it must be alloyed with other metals 1) to secure the required hardness and 2) to create yellow, white, rose, and green gold. While different jewelry manufacturers use different "recipes" to obtain these colors, some of the alloys added to pure gold, in varying percentages, are as follows:

yellow gold	copper and silver
white gold	nickel, silver, zinc, platinum, palladium
rose gold	copper
green gold	silver, zinc, copper

These alloys, not the gold that is usually blamed, may cause problems for those who love to wear gold jewelry. Ear piercing, for example, may cause difficulties. If you follow instructions carefully, most likely you will not have a problem in the six-week period during which you are not to remove the ear-piercing studs. But once the studs have been removed and you begin to wear different kinds of earrings, an allergic reaction may occur from nickel and/or other alloys in the metals.

To prevent a reaction, consider, at least for the first six months or even the first year, wearing only nickel-free earrings or only those with hypo-allergenic posts. Another, although more costly, option for eliminating potential allergic reactions is to have a jeweler coat earring posts with rhodium or palladium which, like pure gold, contain no alloys.

Another problem resulting from inserting pierced earrings may be an infection caused by bacteria either on the posts or your hands. As preventive measures, wash your hands thoroughly before removing and inserting earrings and, to the extent possible, make sure the posts are clean. If a solution is used to clean the earrings, make sure the posts are completely dry. Should an infection develop or an allergic reaction occur after taking all precautionary measures possible, you should consult a physician.

In addition, wearing any gold jewelry may result in skin and/or clothing discolorations caused by certain alloys. While pure gold will not tarnish or discolor skin or clothing, some alloys added to the gold may cause problems. The alloys added to silver may result in the same problem when wearing silver jewelry. The acids in perspiration and/or the ingredients in some cosmetics may react, chemically, with gold and silver alloys, especially nickel. This abrasive reaction results in black smudges that transfer to skin or clothing.

To prevent skin and/or clothing from discoloring or at least to minimize the problem, occasionally remove your jewelry, and wash the skin area with mild soap and warm water. Clean the jewelry often with a soft, dry cloth. Whenever possible, purchase gold jewelry with a higher gold content, since higher karatage means fewer problem-causing alloys, especially nickel and copper.

If you have a problem wearing white gold, try to buy only that which is alloyed with palladium or rhodium, since these metals, like pure gold, should not cause adverse reactions, although the jewelry will be more expensive.

INSURANCE AND APPRAISALS

To have invested substantially, through the years, in your jewelry collection is not unreasonable. If that is the case, you may want to consider having your pieces appraised and securing a jewelry insurance policy, in addition to your homeowner's or renter's coverage.

If you decide to secure additional insurance, three important steps are necessary:

❖ Seek professional appraisals of your more expensive pieces. Find a qualified gemologist who is also a certified appraiser. An accurate appraisal protects you as well as the insurance company and ensures a fair reimbursement should a loss occur. The appraisal will include a valuation to determine the price for which an item could be sold in an appropriate market. Since market prices fluctuate periodically, have items appraised every few years to reflect the changing value. In addition, be certain the appraiser's valuation will support a potential claim in a court of law.

❖ Safely store photos, on the reverse sides of which you have indicated key points of information, and keep these together with bills of sale and appraisals.

❖ Discuss various types of coverage with representatives from at least two insurance companies.

Some important questions you should consider asking before selecting a policy are the following:

❖ What coverage would a policy provide? Against fire? Against theft?

❖ Does the policy include deductibles?

- ❖ How does the company satisfy a claim? In cash? With a replacement piece?

- ❖ Does the policy include exemptions, for example, negligence?

- ❖ What documentation must you provide if you file a claim? Photos? Bills of sale? Appraisals?

- ❖ How does the company satisfy the loss of items that cannot be replaced, for example, heirlooms?

And one final point. Most homeowner or renter insurance policies include separate coverage up to $1,000 for loss or damage to jewelry. In today's market, however, this provides little in the way of replacement.

If you have not had your finer jewelry appraised and insured, this information should help you begin these important processes, but it is intended solely as a guide.

BIBLIOGRAPHY

Bank, 1970: *Precious Stones and Minerals*, F. Warne, New York.

Blakemore, 1971: *The Book of Gold*, Stein and Day Publishers, New York.

Curran, 1961: *A Treasury of Jewels and Gems*, Emerson Books, Inc., New York.

Dragsted, 1975: *Gems and Jewelry*, Macmillan Publishing Co., Inc., New York.

Evans, 1970: *A History of Jewellry* 1100-1870, Boston Book and Art, Publisher, Boston.

Hall, 1994: *Gemstones*, Dorling Kindersley, Ltd., London and New York.

Kunz, 1971 Dover edition: *The Curious Lore of Precious Stones*, Dover Publications, Inc., New York.

Luzzatto-Bilitz, 1969 edition: *Antique Jade*, The Hamlyn Publishing Group Limited, Hamlyn House, The Centre, Feltham, Middlesex.

Matlins & Bonanno, 1993: *Jewelry & Gems The Buying Guide,* Gemstone Press, Woodstock, Vermont.

Pough, 1969: *The Story of Gems and Semiprecious Stones,* Harvey House, New York.

Schumann, 1977: *Gemstones of the World*, Sterling Publishing Co., New York.

INDEX

Numbers with asterisks refer to page(s) with the most information about a gemstone.

A

accessories, jewelry as, 78-9

achroite (tourmaline), 67

agate, 7, 19-20*, 31, 46, 50, 57, 73-5, 77

alexandrite, 3, 7, 20-1*, 73

allergies and other problems, 96, 98-9

alloys, 89, 94-6, 98-9

almandine (garnet), 39

amber, 3, 7, 21-3*, 74, 87

amethyst, 3, 8, 23-4*, 32, 51, 57, 73-6

andalusite, 3, 8, 24-5*

apostles, twelve, 76

appraisals, 100-101

aquamarine, 3, 8, 25-6*, 28, 73, 76

aventurine, 3, 8, 26-7*, 42, 57

azurite, 3, 27-8*

azur-malachite, 9, 27*

B

beryl, 3, 9, 25, 28-9*, 37, 74-6

birthstones, 73-4

bloodstone, 3, 9, 29-30*, 31, 57, 73-4

C

cabochon cut, 83

cameo, 20, 30, 50

carat (CT), 34-5, 54, 85, 88

care and cleaning, 86-8

carnelian, 3, 10, 26, 30-1*, 57, 74-6

chains, 78, 96-7

chalcedony, 3, 10, 19, 29, 30, 31*, 44, 50, 57, 76

chrysoberyl, 20

chrysoprase, 31, 42, 73, 76

citrine, 3, 10, 32*, 57, 74, 76

clarity, 35, 85

clasps, 78-9, 88, 97

color, 3, 19, 71-2, 77, 85

coloration, 86

color plates, gemstone, 7-18, 72

copper, 47, 89, 94, 98

coral, 1, 3, 10, 33*, 74, 76

corundum, 58, 60

crystal, 2, 76

crystal, rock, 73

"C's," the four, 35, 85-6

cubic zirconia (CZ), 11, 34*, 71

cuts, gemstone, 83-5

INDEX (Continued)

D

demantoid (garnet), 39
diamond, 3, 11, 19, 34-6*, 37, 59, 60, 70, 73, 75, 77, 88
diopside, 3, 11, 37*
discoloration,
skin and clothing, 99
doublet, 52
dravite (tourmaline), 67
durability, 19, 86

E

emerald, 3, 11, 19, 25, 28, 37-8*, 39, 51, 56, 73-7

F

faceted cut, 83
feldspar, 49

G

garnet, 3, 12, 38-40*, 73-6
gem, 1, 19, 71-2, 88
gemology,
the science of, 1-2
gemstone, 1, 3, 19, 83, 85, 88
gemstones,
introduction to, 19
gold, 41, 56, 68, 77, 87-9, 93-4, 95-6, 98-9
golden beryl, 9, 28-9*
grossular (garnet), 39

H

hallmark, 94
heliotrope, 29
hessonite (garnet), 39
hues, 3, 72, 85

I

indicolite (tourmaline), 67
insurance, 100-101
iolite, 3, 12, 40-1*
Israel,
twelve tribes of, 75
ivory, 1, 77

J

jade, 3, 12, 41-3*, 62, 74, 77
jadeite, 43
jasper, 12, 29, 31, 44*, 57, 73, 75-6
jewelry, 1, 71, 78-9, 86-8

K

karat (K or KT), 88-9, 94-5
kunzite, 3, 13, 44-5*

L

lapis lazuli, 3, 13, 28, 45-7*, 61, 63, 74
lead, 94

INDEX (Continued)

INDEX (Continued)

BIRTHDAY NOTES

NAME	BIRTHDATE	BIRTHSTONE

BIRTHDAY NOTES

NAME	BIRTHDATE	BIRTHSTONE

ANNIVERSARY NOTES

NAME	DATE	SYMBOL
_____	_____	_____
_____	_____	_____
_____	_____	_____
_____	_____	_____
_____	_____	_____
_____	_____	_____
_____	_____	_____
_____	_____	_____
_____	_____	_____
_____	_____	_____
_____	_____	_____
_____	_____	_____
_____	_____	_____
_____	_____	_____
_____	_____	_____
_____	_____	_____
_____	_____	_____

ANNIVERSARY NOTES

NAME	DATE	SYMBOL

NOTES

NOTES

NOTES

NOTES